Keywords in Policing

CHALLENGING MINDS. INSPIRING SUCCESS.

Keywords in Policing

Ian K. Pepper and Helen Pepper

 Open University Press

Open University Press
McGraw-Hill Education
McGraw-Hill House
Shoppenhangers Road
Maidenhead
Berkshire
England
SL6 2QL

email: enquiries@openup.co.uk
world wide web: www.openup.co.uk

and Two Penn Plaza, New York, NY 10121–2289, USA

First published 2009

A catalogue record of this book is available from the British Library

ISBN–13: 978033522377-0 (pb) 978-033-522376-3 (hb)
ISBN–10: 033522377-X (pb) 033522376-1

Library of Congress Cataloguing-in-Publication Data
CIP data applied for

Typeset by YHT Ltd, London
Printed in the UK by Bell and Bain Ltd, Glasgow

The McGraw·Hill Companies

Dedicated to Laurie and Irene Blake, Brian and Barbara Pepper
and our son Thomas

Introduction: the development of law enforcement and policing across the UK

From their inception, like any other large organization, the law enforcement agencies of the UK have been subject to the development and evolution of their own language and abbreviations ranging from 'Bow Street Runners' and the 'Edmund Davies report' in the early years to 'ADVOKATE', 'DNA boost', 'IPLDP', 'miscarriage of justice', 'NIM' and 'Skills for Justice' in the contemporary service.

The contemporary law enforcement officer operates in a diverse and constantly evolving environment. However, the role, and one therefore assumes specific language, of an officer enforcing the law can be traced back to the Anglo Saxons. Critchley (1967) details how one individual was made responsible for justice over a group of families. These groups of families were overseen by a royal reeve who exercised judicial power who, in turn, was answerable to a local shire reeve who, over time, became referred to as the 'sheriff', a term with which we are familiar today.

With the Norman Conquest of England in the eleventh century, another familiar title and role within contemporary law enforcement was established, that of the constable. They became responsible for gathering intelligence on locals and informing on them to their Norman masters. Towards the end of the thirteenth century the Statute of Winchester established the need for watchmen to patrol the entrances to fortified towns to apprehend strangers. In the mid-sixteenth century the Marian legislation enabled Justices of the Peace to conduct investigations before a trial took place by gathering evidence from victims and offenders (Rawlings 2002).

The eighteenth century saw a great increase in industrialization and urbanization and resultant increases in crime and criminality. Public protest also led to the introduction of legislation in an attempt to deal with moral issues arising such as the Gin Act in 1736 (ibid.); however, such legislation was hard to enforce without a professional enforcement organization. In 1750 two magistrates, John and Henry Fielding, established a group of paid professional constables to investigate and tackle those committing street robberies and murders in London. The constables were based in Bow Street and soon became known as the 'Bow Street Runners', but did not patrol the streets.

In 1798 Patrick Colquhoun, an advocate of a full-time professional police force, established a small force of officers as a private venture to actively patrol and police the port area of London (Critchley 1967). This police force had great success and became a public body in 1800. At a similar time at a number of locations around the country, such as Glasgow and Birmingham, private police forces were being established that would become public bodies.

In 1829, with the driving force of the Home Secretary at the time, Sir Robert Peel, the Metropolitan Police Act established the Metropolitan Police, which at the time, as now, was the largest police force in the country. The Special Constabulary was first established in 1831 and the first detective department was established in Birmingham during 1839 (Rawlings 2002). As trust and confidence in the police began to grow other urban areas established police forces and the 1839 Rural Constabulary Act enabled the development of police forces in more rural areas. By the turn of the twentieth century there were in excess of 250 police forces across the country (Grieve et al. 2007).

In 1901 the first fingerprint bureau to aid in the detection of offenders was established in the Metropolitan Police area. Many police officers enlisted in the military during the 1914–1918 World War I, and following threats of strike action by officers in 1918, the Desborough Committee was established to review police organization, pay and conditions (Fido and Skinner 1999). World War II brought many women, who to a large extent had been ignored as effective police employees, into the police service (Rawlings 2002). In the late 1960s the large number of urban and rural forces were amalgamated to become the 43 Home Office police forces currently in existence across England and Wales today (Grieve et al. 2007). There are also numerous other non-Home Office police forces and a number of forces across Scotland and Northern Ireland (for a complete list see Appendix 1).

Civil unrest in the early 1980s, such as the Brixton riots and a number of high-profile miscarriages of justice, led to legislative reform, such as the enactment of the Police and Criminal Evidence Act (PACE), in 1984. The McPherson report into the murder of Stephen Lawrence in London during 1993 concluded that there was institutional racism and professional incompetence within the police with proposals for the need to reform aspects of police training, culture and the investigation of complaints. Civilianization of non-operational police posts grew throughout the 1990s, and the Police Reform Act (2002) has continued such reforms by increasing partnership working between agencies and creating specific new policing roles, such as community support officers, with further developments formalizing other law enforcement practitioner roles, such as the UK Borders Act (2007) establishing the UK Border Agency. The debate as to whether national policing is the way forward continues to this day and is perhaps a step closer with the creation of the Serious Organized Crime Agency (SOCA) in 2006.

Using this collection of keywords, acronyms, abbreviations and mnemonics

The modern police service is organized into 43 police forces in England and Wales, eight in Scotland, one in Northern Ireland and a number of large geographic forces with specific policing roles (e.g. the Civil Nuclear Constabulary) and a range of smaller specially focused forces (e.g. the Port of Dover Police). There are well over 260 000 employees of the police forces nationwide, not to mention the expanding national law enforcement organizations such as SOCA (Serious Organized Crime Agency) and SCDEA (Scottish Drug Enforcement Agency). As such the specialist subject-specific language that has evolved, and continues to evolve, can be particularly confusing to new or aspiring law enforcement practitioners whatever their role within the wider police family, along with those working with partner organizations or anyone interested in the specific language used by and related to these professional organizations.

This collection of common words used in policing, acronyms (words made from the first letters of a collection of words), abbreviations (shortened words) and mnemonics (a term used to assist in aiding memory) often referred to within police education and training, along with those being used within the operational environment, could never be a complete list. The dynamic nature of policing across numerous and changing law enforcement agencies across the country, along with external influences such as new legislation, would not allow the collection and collation of such a universal compendium.

However, with over 1000 entries this text goes some way towards addressing the challenge of understanding the language presented to new or aspiring regular officers, police community support officers, special constables or one of many other civilian specialist roles such as detention officers, indexers or crime scene investigators. While the text also provides a record of those common keywords, acronyms, abbreviations and mnemonics used across a wide audience of UK law enforcement organizations in the early twenty-first century.

This text describes and cross-references the most common form in which words, acronyms, abbreviations and mnemonics are referred to and used within the police and law enforcement community. It avoids slang, such as 'copper' and 'nicked', and is not intended to provide legal guidance; instead, it provides over 1000 short, easy to access and follow explanations, presented in alphabetical order of the terms used on a regular basis across the contemporary policing and law enforcement family.

A

A1 assessor: an assessor's qualification focused on the assessment of evidence for National Vocational Qualifications (NVQs).

AAIB: Air Accidents Investigation Branch; non-police organization reporting to the Department for Transport. AAIB have specialist skills in the investigation of civil aircraft accidents and incidents. Their aim is to prevent similar accidents occurring in the future but not to apportion blame (AAIB 2006).

ABC: Acceptable Behaviour Contract; a written agreement setting out the behaviour that is acceptable for all the parties concerned including the individual offender, the police and local authority officials (Bullock and Jones 2004) (*see also* **ASBO**).

ABH: actual bodily harm; defined by the Offences Against the Person Act (1861) as any injury that interferes with the health and comfort of the victim.

ABI: Association of British Insurers; represents the common interests of insurers across the UK.

ABM: Area Business Manager; the chief administrator for a Basic Command Unit (BCU).

ACC: assistant chief constable; a high-ranking police officer.

accelerants: anything that is used to intentionally speed up the growth of a fire, examples of which could be petrol or hay.

accelerated promotion scheme: a fast-track promotion scheme for those police candidates who show aptitude and promise. After a good grounding in police work an officer would expect to reach the rank of inspector within seven years (*see also* **HPDS**).

accountability: at the level of each police force the organization is held accountable for its actions through a tripartite system of governance consisting of the Home Office, responsible for ensuring the efficiency of the police and the provision of national key objectives, the chief constable, responsible for direction and control, including effective management of the force's budget, and the police authority, responsible for community consultation, setting a local policing plan to meet the local needs and monitoring of how it is achieved. Each year reports are sent to the Home Secretary by the chief constable and the police authority detailing how effectively targets set have been achieved. Her Majesty's Inspectorate of Constabulary (HMIC), through inspections of police forces and thematic reviews (e.g. police training), adds an extra aspect of accountability, although as HMIC report to the Home Secretary, it could be argued that they actually provide an additional element of Home Office control. At the level of individual police officers, McLaughlin (2007) suggests that through legislation, police officers (and one would add in subsequent years police community support officers) have been given powers and the discretion on when to use them to intervene in the lives of others. As well as being accountable directly to their line managers, who can initiate proceedings against the police discipline codes, and of course the prosecution of police officers for the commission of a criminal act, additional checks on serious infringements of police powers can be investigated by the Independent Police Complaints Commission (IPCC) (*see also* **IPCC**, **Regulation 9 notice** and **Regulation 13**).

ACE CARD: a mnemonic relating to a model designed to assist law enforcement officers when approaching the scene of a collision. The officer should carefully work through the following: **A** – Approach the collision from the rear in a safe manner; **C** – Caution signs should be displayed to oncoming vehicles (never turn your back to the oncoming vehicles); **E** – Examine the scene of the collision briefly in order to make an assessment; **C** – Casualties and their needs should be considered; **A** – Ambulance, fire and other services (e.g. the Highways Agency) should be requested if required; **R** – Remove obstructions in order to reopen the road; **D** – Detailed investigation must be conducted (NCPE 2006).

ACE-V: term used in the comparison of fingerprints meaning that the fingerprints have been **A**nalysed, **C**ompared, **E**valuated and **V**erified by fingerprint examiners.

ACPO: Association of Chief Police Officers; a professional association for senior police officers in England, Wales and Northern Ireland. ACPO provides professional opinions on key policing matters.

ACPOS: Association of Chief Police Officers Scotland; a professional association for senior police officers in Scotland.

Acquitted: the finding of a person not guilty by a criminal court.

Actus reus: the physical wrongful act of committing a crime (*see also* **Mens rea**).

Activity-based costing: a business management tool that in policing terms allows a cost to be calculated for policing a certain area.

ADAT: Alcohol and Drug Action Team; a multi-agency group responsible for the strategic planning of responses to alcohol- and drug-related incidents within a certain geographical area.

ADVOKATE: a mnemonic for officers to use when talking to a witness to try and elicit information from them about a suspect. The mnemonic stands for: **A**mount of time the suspect was watched by the witness; **D**istance between the witness and the suspect; **V**isibility between the witness and suspect; **O**bstructions between the witness and suspect; **K**nown or seen before; **A**nything that stood out about the suspect that helped the witness remember him or her; **T**ime from when the suspect was first seen by the witness; **E**rrors between descriptions (*see also* **Turnbull Rule**).

AEP: Attenuating Energy Projectile (*see* **Baton round**).

AFIS: Automatic Fingerprint Identification System; searchable computer databases that have the ability to compare fingerprints taken from suspects with known offenders and crime scene marks. Komarinski (2005) suggests that the FBI probably has the largest AFIS database holding in excess of 46 million records (*see also* **Ident 1**).

AFO: authorized firearms officer; police officer permitted to carry firearms (*see also* **ARV**, **Firearm** and **Tactical Firearms Unit**).

AFR: Automatic Fingerprint Recognition, computerized fingerprint identification system.

AIB: Accident Investigation Branch; specialist personnel with skill in the investigation of road traffic collisions and vehicle defects.

Airwave: a secure digital radio network using similar technology to mobile telephones for use by the police and other emergency services for communication between their control room and themselves (*see also* **Airwave Status Codes**, **Control Room** and **PSRCS**).

Airwave status codes: a series of nationally recognized numbered codes that enable law enforcement officers to swiftly communicate their status to their colleagues without lengthy radio communication, such as the transmission of the number '1' would show they are on duty, '6' would show they are at a scene and '32' would indicate they are involved in neighbourhood policing (*see also* **Airwave**).

A/L: annual leave; yearly holiday entitlement.

ALF: Animal Liberation Front; animal rights activist group.

ALI: Adult Learning Inspectorate; a non-departmental public body responsible for inspecting all work-based education and training.

Alibi: when charged with a criminal offence, the accused suggests that he or she was elsewhere at the time the offence was committed.

Alpha: a letter of the phonetic alphabet that is utilized to describe the letter A (*see* **Appendix 4**).

Aluminium powder: a silver-coloured flake powder used by CSIs to locate fingerprints.

Amphetamines: an illegal synthetic drug used as a stimulant, usually found as a powder in paper wraps but can also be discovered in tablet or capsule form. As a powder it is normally white, although it has been encountered as a pink powder. It has a very distinctive ammonia-like smell, which is often described as being like cat urine. The correct name is amphetamine sulphate, and this is the name used when formulating a charge. Street names include speed, whizz or uppers. Amphetamine can be swallowed, sniffed or smoked, but the most common method of abuse is to dissolve it in water and inject it. It is a neurological stimulant, increasing levels of alertness and energy, and allowing extended periods without sleep. It is also an appetite suppressant, so is sometimes abused as an aid to weight loss. It is known to cause mood swings, aggression and insomnia leading to exhaustion. It is used therapeutically to treat Attention Deficit Hyperactivity Disorder (ADHD) and some sleep disorders such as narcolepsy. Its effect of increasing alertness and aiding concentration led to it being used by soldiers during World War II, and also abused by students as a study aid.

ANACAPA: commercially designed knowledge-based analytical techniques used in the investigation of complex criminal activities, in order to visualize the position of the investigation, extract meanings from this and thus create useful operational intelligence (*see also* **Crime pattern analysis, Five × five intelligence, Intelligence, Intelligence analyst, Intelligence cycle, NIM** and **Watson**).

Animal hair brush: soft brush for the application of granular black and white fingerprint powder.

ANPR: Automatic Number Plate Recognition; mobile computerized number plate system used to compare details in its memory.

Anthropology: *see* **Forensic anthropology.**

Anthropometry: anthropometry is the science of taking and applying quantitative measurement of the human body for the purpose of comparison. Alphonse Bertillon devised a system in the late nineteenth century for classifying and identifying criminals based on a series of measurements of the body, such as their height, length of ring finger and breadth of head, and so on. This system of identification was largely superseded with the introduction of fingerprint identification techniques. In the late 1990s measurements of the body, or biometrics, have once more come to the fore with the technological advances allowing the use of information technology (IT) to scan and compare different parts of the body ranging from fingerprints to the retina (*see also* **Biometrics** and **Galton, Francis**).

AOAB: Assault Occasioning Actual Bodily Harm; defined under section 47 of the Offences Against the Person Act (1861) as when someone intentionally, or through their reckless actions, hurts an individual in a way that affects their health or well-being in a less than serious way.

APA: Association of Police Authorities; represents police authorities across England, Wales and Northern Ireland. Each policing area must have a police authority, that is in place to ensure efficient and effective policing within that area.

ARCC: Aeronautical Rescue Coordination Centre; operated by the Royal Air Force from a base in Scotland, and working closely with the other emergency services, ARCC deploys and coordinates aeronautical assets, and the RAF Mountain Rescue Team, to a range of incidents including saving lives.

Arch: A pattern made up of the ridges found on a thumb or finger (*see also* **Fingerprints**).

Archaeology: *see* **Forensic archaeology**.

Architectural liaison officer: sometimes called 'crime prevention design officers', ALOs act as a point of contact within the police for professionals who are designing and building with consideration for reducing crime and the fear of crime within their premises (*see also* **CPO, Crime prevention through environmental design** and **Situational crime prevention**).

Arrest: depriving an individual of his or her liberty.

Arrest summons number (ASN): the number issued by the police national computer to uniquely identify a defendant in a case (*see also* **Phoenix sourced document** and **PNC**).

Arson: defined in the Criminal Damage Act (1971), arson is the damage or destruction by fire of property belonging to someone else.

ARV: armed response vehicle; specialist firearms-equipped personnel in a mobile unit (*see also* **AFO, Firearm** and **Tactical Firearms Unit**).

ASBAT: Anti-Social Behaviour Action Team; a multidisciplinary team that aims to resolve serious cases of anti-social behaviour through partnership resolutions with organizations, such as schools, housing associations and the council.

ASBO: Anti-Social Behaviour Order; originally established as part of the Crime and Disorder Act (1998). An ASBO is an order prohibiting offenders from committing anti-social acts or entering certain defined areas. An ASBO is designed to protect the general public from behaviours that cause or may cause distress (*see also* **ABC**).

ASBO 13: Anti-Social Behaviour Order – warning; a form completed and issued by law enforcement officers prior to an ASBO, warning individuals of an offence with copies of the form sent to parents/guardians and the school.

ASCLD: American Society of Crime Laboratory Directors; a professional society.

ASN: *see* **Arrest summons number**.

ASP: police issue baton (similar to a truncheon) used by a police officer for restraining individuals and his or her own defence (*see also* **Baton** and **Truncheon**).

Asphyxia: a significant interference with the intake of oxygen and exhalation of carbon dioxide from the human body leading to death (*see also* **Hypoxia**).

Assets Recovery Agency: the Assets Recovery Agency was established in 2003 as a result of the 2002 Proceeds of Crime Act with an aim of damaging organized criminal activity and recovering the proceeds of crime.

Assistant Commissioner: a senior police rank in the Metropolitan Police.

ASU: Air Support Unit or Administrative Support Unit; ASUs are operated by a number of police forces across the UK using a range of types of helicopter, such as the purpose-designed Eurocopter EC135, and to a lesser extent that fixed-wing aircraft, such as the Britten-Norman Defender. These aircraft are usually crewed by a civilian pilot and two police observers with specialist equipment. The ASU can provide an 'eye in the sky' and a communications centre in order to support policing operations. Some of the aircraft are owned by the police authorities; others are leased (*see also* **FLIR**). ASUs are operated by the majority of police forces to provide specialist civilian administrative and clerical support to front-line policing ranging from the transcription of taped interviews to the assessment of prosecution files and the updating of NSPIS.

AVCIS: ACPO Vehicle Crime Intelligence Service; established under the guidance of ACPO in 2006 and centrally based within the UK. The aim of

AVCIS is to work with partners to investigate and disrupt vehicle crime across the country while gathering intelligence on vehicles and their use across all types of crime (ACPO Vehicle Crime Intelligence Service 2008) (*see also* **SVS**).

B

Bail: when an individual is released from the custody of the police or the courts pending the individual presenting himself or herself at a criminal court or at a police station.

Bailiff: the County Courts Act 1888 provides for the appointment of one or more high bailiffs. The duty of the high bailiff is to serve all summonses and orders, and execute all warrants, precepts and writs issued out of the court. The High bailiffs can appoint as many bailiffs as they need to assist in their duties.

Ballistics: the study of firearms; usually divided into three areas of study: internal ballistics (what happens within the firearm when it is fired and as the bullet travels down the barrel), external ballistics (this is essentially concerned with the flight of the bullet); and terminal ballistics (what happens as the bullet ends its flight impacting a surface and the resultant effects). The forensic study of ballistics by firearms experts can provide law enforcement agencies with invaluable evidence, such as the identification of the firearm used, the approximation of the location of the shooter and, after examination within a laboratory, the ability to link bullets and cartridge cases to the firearm from which they were discharged (*see also* **Firearm**, **Forensic firearms** and **NaBID**).

Barrister: a legal professional who specializes in representing a client within either a civil or criminal court (*see* **Queens Counsel**).

Baseline assessment process: an open assessment of policing that resulted in league tables of performance comparing forces.

Baton: used by a police officer for restraining individuals and his or her own defence (*see also* **ASP** and **Truncheon**).

Baton round: a less than lethal large calibre weapon used as an alternative to using a firearm that has potentially deadly outcomes. The baton round was first introduced in the 1970s, although associated with civil disturbance in Northern Ireland; rounds have been fired in England and Wales. They can only be used by specially trained and authorized firearms officers and will knock over and stun an individual at a range of 20 metres or so, but they are not always 100 per cent effective (Rogers 2003). Baton rounds have also unfortunately killed individuals when they have been hit in vulnerable areas such as the head. After much research baton rounds have now been replaced by AEP (attenuating energy projectile) rounds that aim to achieve the same result but more safely (*see also* **Taser**).

BAWP: British Association of Women in Policing; an association aimed at enhancing the role and profile of women within policing.

BCS: British Crime Survey; first conducted in 1982 and now researched annually on behalf of the government, the BCS measures crime in England and Wales by surveying people about the crimes of which they have been victims, including those that are not reported to the police. The BCS also supplies data on those at risk of criminal activities, attitudes towards crime and the whole criminal justice system, thus providing alternative data to that supplied by the police statistics (Home Office 2006a).

BCU: Basic Command Unit; termed 'Boroughs' in the Metropolitan Police Force, each force area is divided into a number of BCUs for operational policing, the boundaries of which usually align themselves to those of the local authority. BCUs are usually headed by a superintendent (*see also* **OCU**).

Benchmarking: the comparison of the performance of different units within a force or different forces carrying out similar tasks in similar situations where the outputs can be measured. Examples range from the reduction of street crime to the identification of fingerprints recovered from crime scenes.

Bertillon, Alphonse: a late-nineteenth and early twentieth-century French police employee who devised a system for classifying and identifying criminals based on a series of measurements of the body (*see also* **Anthropometry**).

Bichard: a report, chaired by Michael Bichard, published in 2005. The report researched how the investigation into the murders in Soham of the children Jessica Chapman and Holly Wells by Ian Huntley were conducted by the police and criminal justice agencies. It examined the sharing of information between police forces and the vetting of those working with children and those who would be deemed vulnerable (*see also* **Independent Safeguarding Authority** and **MoPI**).

Bikesafe/Bikewise: a national initiative in relation to the motorbike community aiming to reduce the number of collisions, deaths and injuries on the roads (*see* **Roads Policing Unit**).

Binding over: a magistrates court may require a person to keep the peace or be of good behaviour for a set period of time.

Biohazard: a biological hazard to health such as blood or other body fluids (*see also* **Biohazard bag** and **Health and safety**).

Biohazard bag: a bag or container used to place items for disposal that may have come into contact with blood or other body fluids (*see also* **Biohazard**).

Biometrics: generally held to be the use of technology to identify an individual through the mathematical analysis of a biological feature (e.g. facial recognition or fingerprints) in order to restrict entry and/or access to secure areas in airports, banks, computer hardware, and so on (*see also* **Anthropometry, FIND** and **Fingerprints**).

Black powder: a black-coloured granular powder used by CSIs to locate fingerprints.

Body armour: a generic term used to describe the PPE provided to police officers in the form of a protective vest. Law enforcement agencies conduct risk assessments in line with Home Office guidance to ensure that they provide the correct level of protection to the major organs of the body in relation to the likelihood of the officer being exposed to attack with a knife or spike to a firearm (*see also* **PPE**).

Body bag: a new, clean, sturdy bag used to place the body of a deceased in order to preserve forensic evidence, prior to the removal of the body to a mortuary from the scene of the sudden or unexplained death.

Bogus caller: *see* **Distraction burglary**.

BOMB ALERT: a mnemonic for remembering the key requirements to consider when responding to a suspicious package that may be a bomb: **B**uildings to be evacuated, **O**ccupants moved away to safety, **M**ove onlookers away from the scene, **B**ack away (consider the possibility of secondary devices), **A**ccurate information should be communicated back to the control room, **L**ocate and get details of potential witnesses, **E**vacuate surrounding areas, **R**endezvous point established and communicated, **T**ape off the area to establish appropriate cordons (*see also* **EOD**).

Border Agency: an executive agency of the Home Office. The UK Border Agency was established in 2008 under the UK Borders Act (2007) taking responsibility for managing migration, customs, applications to visit or live in the UK, along with applications for asylum (UKBA 2008) (*see also* **Ports Officer** and **Special Branch**).

Bow Street Runners: an eighteenth-century group of paid constables based in Bow Street, established by the brothers Henry and John Fielding to tackle the robbery and murder gangs operating in London. Also known as the 'thief takers' (*see also* **Constable** and **Fielding, John and Henry**).

Boxing: when a series of police vehicles driven by specially trained police officers 'box in' and gradually slow down a vehicle bringing it to a stop (*see also* **Pursuit, Roads Policing Unit** and **Rolling block**).

BPA: Black Police Association; an association established in 1994 for black and Asian members of the police force.

Bravo: a letter of the phonetic alphabet that is utilized to describe the letter B (*see* **Appendix 4**).

Breach of the peace: a breach of the peace can occur when harm is done or is likely to be done to a person or property and in some circumstances is in fear of such harm.

Broken windows: a theory first brought to the fore in the 1980s where a neighbourhood can descend into disorder and then crime if standards of maintenance, such as not repairing smashed windows or clearing up graffiti, are seen as a signal to potential offenders that the community has lost interest and does not really care about the environment where they live and work (*see also* **Zero Tolerance**).

Bronze commander: the individual commander who takes operational control at the scene of an incident in order to control and deploy resources from their own emergency service, thus also called the operational commander (*see also* **Silver commander, Gold commander** and **Golden hour**).

BS799: British Standard for Information Security Management.

BTP: the British Transport Police have responsibility for policing the rail network, London Underground and other associated areas (*see* **Appendix 1**).

Buccal cells: Buccal cells are found within saliva and contain the DNA of the donor. It is the buccal cells that are sampled when a non-intimate sample (defined under the Police and Criminal Evidence Act 1984) is taken in the form of swabs scraped over the inside of the cheek of a person in custody (*see also* **DNA, Non-intimate samples** and **Plucked head hair**).

Buccal swab: *see* **Buccal cells**.

Bumblebee, operation: a Metropolitan Police operation first commenced in 1991 and is still operable today. The focus of the operation is to reduce burglary and the fear of crime across the Metropolitan Police area, but its impact has spread to areas far beyond this.

Burglary: defined in the Theft Act (1968), burglary has many forms including aggravated burglary, but generally revolves around the offender entering premises as a trespasser with the intention of committing an offence.

BVPI: Best Value Performance Indicator; instigated by the Audit Commission during the 1990s, the police service now needs to demonstrate how it achieves the best value for its money. BVPI is a method of collecting data that may be used for the purpose of best value review (*see also* **Offence code**).

Byford Report: the 1981 report by Sir Lawrence Byford into the investigation of the 13 murders and 7 attempted murders committed by the 'Yorkshire Ripper'. The enquiry concluded that there were errors and inefficiencies in the conduct of the investigation and made a number of recommendations including the importance of corporate management, improved training, improved major incident room procedures and computerization, one senior investigating officer (SIO) for series crimes and improved scientific support. As a result of the recommendation to improve scientific support the role of 'Byford Scientist' was established as a specialist forensic science adviser taking a strategic view of all forensic submissions in a major enquiry and responsible for liaison between the forensic laboratory and the SIO (*see also* **HOLMES II, MIRSAP, Serial killer** and **SIO**).

C

CAD: Computer Aided Dispatch; an IT solution to the creation of records in real time by a controller adding more detailed information to that added into the CAD system, such as a caller's number. The system also tracks the deployment of law enforcement personnel along with the interrogation of existing information held by the agency, such as wanted people or stolen vehicles.

CADDIE: Crime and Disorder Data Information Exchange; a web-based resource first piloted in 2001 and now used to share and exchange information between agencies involved in dealing with crime and disorder.

C&C: command and control; the direction provided by a designated commander (or commanders in the case of a multi-agency operation) ensuring that personnel, equipment, communications, facilities and procedures are used to their best ability to ensure success.

C&D: complaints and discipline; a police department responsible for the conduct of internal police investigations relating to complaints against the police and disciplinary procedures; also known as professional standards department.

Cannabis: an illegal drug from a plant called Cannabis sativa that comes in several forms but is almost always smoked, in large, loosely hand-rolled cigarettes known as joints or roaches, or in pipes or bongs. Cannabis can also be used in cooking or baking, or drunk as a tea. It is also referred to as marijuana or ganja. The most commonly encountered form is resin, which is scraped from the plant and then compressed into blocks, often known as nine bars because they weigh nine ounces. The colour of the resin varies depending on its country of origin, from black (Pakistani black) through to a pale sandy brown (Lebanese gold). The smallest amount of cannabis resin sold on the street would be a sixteenth of an ounce, a cube of resin with sides of approximately one centimetre. However, because cannabis resin is cheap and easily available it is not unusual for users to buy an ounce at a time. Cannabis is also found in herbal form (dried plant material) or, rarely, in a concentrated liquid form known as hash oil. 'Skunk' cannabis is a genetically enhanced form that is grown hydroponically on indoor cannabis farms. The active compound in cannabis is tetrahydrocannabinol (THC); in cannabis resin the THC content is normally around 6–8 per cent, but in skunk it can be as high as 15 per cent.

Cannabis warning: after a review of elements of the Drugs Act (2005) by the Home Office in 2006, a decision was reached that if a person 18 or over is found to have in their possession a small amount of cannabis without any intention to supply the drug, then this could be dealt with by disposal outside of the court in the form of a cannabis warning. This warning must be accompanied by the officer making complete and accurate records of the warning (*see also* **Out of court disposal**).

Canteen culture: the grouping together of individuals, in this case within the police canteen, will inevitably lead to the establishment of a sub-culture. In this respect the police have a sub-culture in which they 'hide away' from the dangers of the outside world for mutual defence (Waddington 1999) and this isolation assists police officers in developing resolutions to shared problems. Skolnick (1966) identifies some of the main aspects of the police sub-culture as suspiciousness, internal isolation and solidarity. There is still however little empirical research to demonstrate that what occurs in the canteen directly influences what occurs on the streets; instead, the police canteen sub-culture could just have been created by the media for their own purposes (Waddington 1999).

CAP: common approach path; the route taken by the first police officers attending the scene of a crime, which then becomes the route that the entire emergency services' personnel will use within the crime scene to enter and leave. This should be the route least likely to have been taken by an offender and as such will assist with the preservation of the evidence present.

Case file: the collection of MG forms and reports relating to a specific case collated by the officer in the case and submitted to the Crown Prosecution Service for the prosecution of the case (*see also* **CPS** and **MG forms**).

Casualty Bureau: a casualty bureau is a central point for recording information relating to people who have or may have been involved in a disaster or major incident that is likely to have involved numerous casualties. All the information received, which includes names, descriptions, and so on, must be collated and processed, and then disseminated to the law enforcement personnel conducting the inquiry. The casualty bureau also acts as a central point of contact for friends and relatives of people who may have been caught up in the incident, through the issue to the public, usually via the media, of a contact telephone number.

Casualty Reduction Scheme: a partnership scheme that involves the Police, Local Authorities, Highways Agency and the courts in each force area working in a coordinated manner to respond to the need to reduce the number of deaths and serious injuries on the roads. This could, for example, include targeted road safety campaigns, the deployment of speed cameras and/or the reviewing of road markings.

Caution: when a person is being arrested the caution is used by the law enforcement officer to explain to them in a simple and straightforward way that they are being detained and that they do not have to say anything, but also making them aware that whatever they say or do not say may be used in a court of law.

CBRNE: Chemical, biological, radiological and nuclear explosions. The use of any of the above types of weapon to commit a crime, most likely terrorist in nature, is a constant threat of which law enforcement agencies must be aware and plan to respond to. For example, in the autumn of 2001 anthrax spores were found to have been released within the US postal system. This attack led to the deaths of five people, the injury of many more and preventative measures being taken by thousands of US workers.

CCRC: *see* **Criminal Cases Review Commission**.

CCTV: closed circuit television; the Government has invested heavily in CCTV nationally and research suggests that its use has the effect of reducing property crime, such as burglary and also has an effect on those likely to commit crimes such as assaults or vandalism (Brown 1995). However, the reduction in assaults could also be due to the timely deployment of police resources as a result of effective surveillance via CCTV. Case study research concludes that some crimes are reduced and others can be displaced (ibid.). Research conducted on 60 offenders on their decision-making process as to whether to commit a property crime is supportive of these findings. This supportive research identifies that the use of devices such as CCTV assists in the reduction of crime, but only because the likely offender moves to an alternative target (Tunnell 1992). There is also an increase in public confidence of their own safety from the perceived surveillance from CCTV (*see also* **Surveillance**).

CCU: Corporate Communications Unit or Computer Crime Unit; the Corporate Communications Unit is responsible for the coordination of communications both internally and externally to the organization (e.g. the media) (*see also* **Media Advisory Group**). The Computer Crime Unit is responsible for advising officers how to deal with crimes involving IT and the investigation of hi-tech crimes (*see also* **Cybercrime**).

CDRP: Crime and Disorder Reduction Partnership; established as a result of the Crime and Disorder Act 1998, partnerships were established between the police, local authorities, health authorities, probation service, voluntary organizations and businesses aimed at reducing crime and disorder in their area. This was to be achieved through a process of consultation with stakeholders, strategy creation and partnership working.

Cell: a secure place for the safe detention of a suspect (*see also* **Custody suite**).

Central Criminal Court: also known as the 'Old Bailey', the Central Criminal Court is a Crown Court sitting within the City of London.

Central Ticket Office: a department within each police force that deals with the administration of all fixed penalty notices issued both in person by a law enforcement officer and those recorded by traffic enforcement cameras (*see also* **FPN**).

CENTREX: Central Police Training and Development Authority; the part of the police service specializing in meeting the training requirements of the service across England and Wales. In April 2007 CENTREX was merged into the National Police Improvement Agency (NPIA).

CEOPC: Child Exploitation Online Protection Centre; a partnership bringing together law enforcement specialists from the Police, NSPCC and internet businesses and organizations (Jewkes 2007). CEOPC is part of a global network used to fight internet crime against children (e.g. inappropriate online images of children) (*see also* **Child Protection Unit, NHTCU** and **NSLEC**).

CHALET: a mnemonic for remembering the key requirements to communicate to others when responding to a major incident. **C**hemical hazards present, **H**azards to be aware of, **A**ccess to and from the area, **L**ocation details, **E**mergency Services required at the scene, **T**ime of incident.

Charge desk: a counter within the custody suite, often raised above floor level, where a police officer would present a person who he or she has arrested to the custody officer to explain why the person has been arrested so that the custody officer can decide if the person should be detained (*see also* **Custody officer** and **Custody suite**).

Charlie: a letter of the phonetic alphabet that is utilized to describe the letter C (*see* **Appendix 4**).

Chassis number: a unique identifying number found on the bodywork of motor vehicles, caravans and trailers (*see also* **Engine number, VIN** and **VRM**).

CHEMET: chemical meteorological data; in the case of an unexpected atmospheric pollution caused by the release of chemicals, the meteorological office will provide the emergency services with a weather forecast (Met Office 2007) (*see also* **HAZCHEM** and **PACRAM**).

Chief Constable: top police officer rank outside of London.

Chief Inspector: police officer rank.

Chief Superintendent: police officer rank.

Child: for the purposes of policing, a child is generally deemed to be a person who has yet to reach the age of 14.

Child destruction: this is an offence committed when someone intentionally destroys a child capable of being born alive, either at or before birth and before it has an existence independent of its mother.

Child Protection Unit: a unit of police detectives specially trained to investigate crimes against children (*see also* **CEOPC** and **CPT**).

CHIP: Chemicals (Hazard Information and Packaging for Supply) Regulations; health and safety regulations that relate to the correct packaging and storage of chemicals such as those used in the Fingerprint Development Laboratory (FDL).

CHIS: Covert Human Intelligence Source; defined under the Regulation of Investigatory Powers Act 2000, a CHIS is a person who establishes and/or maintains a relationship with an individual for the purposes of obtaining information (*see also* **HUMINT**).

Chromosomes: part of a biological cell containing DNA; humans have 46 chromosomes in each cell (*see also* **DNA**).

Chrystal meth: the street name for methamphetamine, a drug that is prescribed for the treatment of attention deficit hyperactivity disorder (ADHD). When abused it produces effects of euphoria and excitement and is addictive. It can lead to hallucinations, paranoia and psychotic behaviour. It can also result in obsessive cleaning or tidying, but for many the biggest bonus is the sense of sexual liberation. Its ability to keep users awake and feeling good for long periods have resulted in the drug becoming popular on the US dance scene, although its use is still rare in the UK.

CICA: Criminal Injuries Compensation Authority; the CICA administers criminal injuries compensation to those who have been victims of violent crime.

CID: Criminal Investigation Department; a department of plain-clothes detectives who are synonymous with the investigation of crime. The first CID was established in Birmingham during 1839 (Rawlings 2002) (*see also* **Designated investigator, ICIDP, IO, MIT, SIO** and **TI**).

CIS: crime information system; an integrated police IT system.

Civil Contingencies Secretariat: established in 2001 the Civil Contingencies Secretariat works with many partner agencies across the UK in an attempt to ensure that risks to security and safety are identified and managed while maintaining the ability to deal with and recover from emergencies (e.g. foot and mouth) in a timely manner (UK Resilience 2007).

Civil enforcement officer: an individual employed by the council, or a subcontracted commercial company, who is responsible as part of a team for the enforcement of parking regulations (e.g. the issuing of parking tickets).

Civil Nuclear Constabulary: the Civil Nuclear Constabulary (CNC) has responsibility for policing atomic energy and associated establishments across the UK and the security of nuclear materials when they are being transported (*see* **Appendix 1**).

Civilian detention officer: civilian detention officers work within the custody area of a police station dealing with those individuals held within the care of the police. Their duties revolve around ensuring the welfare of those in detention and the associated administrative tasks.

CJA: Criminal Justice Act; the CJA of 1967 was one of the first major reforms of the criminal justice system aimed at streamlining the police, court and penal procedures. Regularly updated, the Criminal Justice Act of 2003 continues this modernization and streamlining process to include the CPS and the needs of victims, witnesses and the community.

CJA label: *see* **Exhibit label**.

CJPOA: Criminal Justice and Public Order Act 1994; a wide-ranging act aimed at updating criminal offences specifically in the areas felt by the Home Secretary to be lacking in restriction. The act continues to cause controversy as it affects gatherings for rave parties, a suspect's right to silence and the creation of a national DNA database.

CJSU: Criminal Justice Support Unit; using administrative skills, the CJSU collect and collate original case notes from operational staff and then build the case file for submission and disclosure to the CPS and the Defence.

CJSSS: simple, speedy and summary justice; a system of practices and procedures aimed at improving the way in which cases are managed and dealt with between varying justice agencies within the criminal justice system.

CLDP: Core Leadership Development Programme; a formal programme designed to develop leadership and equip leaders with the skills appropriate to their role. The programme is delivered across the police service from constables to chief officers.

Clerk to the court: an administrative role within the courts. The clerk to the court will organize and manage the trial, ensuring that the correct people are in the right place at the right time (*see also* **Usher**).

Close Protection Unit: specially trained officers responsible for the protection of an individual or group (e.g. politicians or royalty) from physical harm or kidnap (*see also* **Diplomatic Protection Group**).

CMU: Crime Management Unit; a unit responsible for the day-to-day allocation and monitoring of investigations into crimes that may extend across numerous departments and specialists.

CNC: *see* **Civil Nuclear Constabulary**.

Cocaine: an illegal drug, it is found in the form of a shiny white powder that is obtained from the leaves of the coca plant. Cocaine hydrochloride is used therapeutically as a topical anaesthetic, mainly in eye, nose and throat surgery. Cocaine is a popular recreational drug that is usually sniffed or 'snorted' up the nose through a tube such as a drinking straw or rolled-up bank note. The drug is absorbed through the mucous membranes in the nose and induces feelings of euphoria and hyperactivity. Sexual interest and pleasure can also be increased. Effects are felt within 15 minutes of taking the drug and can last from 20 minutes to several hours. After-effects can be depression and a craving to experience the drug again. It is highly addictive, and tolerance is built up rapidly (within hours) (*see also* **Crack cocaine**).

Code of Conduct: established by the Police (Conduct) Regulations 2004, Regulation 3 sets out guidance on the behaviours expected of a police officer in relation to honesty and integrity, fairness and impartiality, politeness and tolerance, the use of force and abuse of authority, the performance of duties, carrying out lawful orders, confidentiality, the commission of criminal acts, protection of property, sobriety, appearance and general conduct (*see* **Regulation 9 notice**).

Code of Ethics: a framework established by some forces that provides guidance on acceptable ethical behaviour and a decision-making process for officers when they take action (Newburn et al. 2007) (*see also* **Discretion**).

Code of Practice: a common set of standards issued by a professional body providing guidance and interpretation on how to complete a specific task or set of tasks.

Cognitive interview: a type of interviewing adopted by the police that is a well-proven method of gathering good quality information from a compliant witness and/or victim (Dando et al. 2008) (*see also* **Interview, PEACE** and **Reid Technique**).

Cold case review: the review of an old criminal case that has remained undetected where either new information has become available or, more commonly, forensic techniques have developed allowing forensic evidence to be re-examined (*see also* **MIT**).

Cold spots: areas identified by intelligence analysts using analytical tools as being low and reduced concentrations of particular types of crime (*see also* **Hotspots** and **Intelligence analyst**).

Colquhoun, Patrick: a magistrate and advocate of a full-time professional police force in late eighteenth-century London. In 1798 he led the establishment of a small force of officers as a private venture partly funded by shipping merchants to actively patrol and police the port area of London (Critchley 1967). In 1800 an Act of Parliament made the force a public body (*see also* **Fielding, John and Henry** and **Peel, Robert**).

Commander: Metropolitan Police officer rank.

Commissioner: the highest ranking Metropolitan Police officer.

Committal: a preliminary enquiry into an offence conducted by magistrates to identify if the case can be dealt with at one court or at a higher court. Committal can also be to a higher court for sentencing.

Common Law: laws based on custom and practice within society.

Community-oriented policing (COP): a method of policing that aims to deal with the issues of most concern to the local community. Dobrin (2006) suggests that COP is proactive in its approach dealing with crime and the fear of crime, while building strong relationships within the community and with other partners and hence increasing the flow of information between the agencies involved and the community itself in order to deal with issues, making an arrest being a final option (*see also* **Intelligence-led policing, Neighbourhood policing, Plural policing** and **Problem-oriented policing**).

Community placement: as part of the Initial Police Learning and Development Programme (IPLDP), police officers under training are attached for a period of time to a local community group (e.g. a youth group) to gain a better understanding of their specific issues and to develop an officer's ability to interact with the specific area of the community (*see also* **IPLDP, Probationer police officer** and **SOLAP**).

Compulsory substance misuse testing: under the Police (Amendment) Regulations 2005, it became legally possible for forces to have police officers tested for the misuse of drugs, to extend such testing to civilian staff in vulnerable or critical roles and to screen applicants for employment (ACPO 2007a).

Confession: when a suspect makes an admission to a person within the guidelines of the law, which incriminates himself or herself (Hannibal and Mountford 2002).

Confidential: if information containing the word 'confidential' (e.g. a completed statement) was revealed to an unauthorized person, it would prejudice the interests of that individual or the organization (*see also* **Disclosure, Restricted, Secret** and **Top secret**).

Consent: a legal term that may be used by a defendant to imply a lawful excuse for committing a crime. Informed consent applies to an individual performing a particular action (e.g. taking fingerprint impressions) being fully aware of the possible consequences.

Constable: although with its routes in eleventh-century Britain, the role of the contemporary police constable can be traced back to the mid-eighteenth century when two magistrates created a small band of skilled paid constables to act as 'thief takers' operating from their offices in Bow Street, London. At the end of the eighteenth century a force of full-time paid police officers were recruited to police the West India Docks in London, although it could be argued that this was in part a private police force as it was initially partially funded by the shipping merchants (Critchley 1967). In 1829 the Metropolitan Police Act, championed by Sir Robert Peel, established the Metropolitan Police followed in the 1830s with a number of other municipal police forces. The police constable today affirms to serve the Queen with fairness, integrity, diligence and impartiality while upholding fundamental human rights and respect for all, with the aim of the preservation of life and property along with the prevention and detection of crime (*see also* **Bow Street Runners, Fielding, John and Henry, PC, Peel, Robert** and **Probationer police officer**).

Contamination: corruption of evidence taking place at either the crime scene or laboratory due to incorrect or poor packaging, inappropriate practices, such as coughing over samples, or secondary transfer, such as allowing evidence to be exchanged between the suspect and the victim's clothes when they are both transported in the same police vehicle but at different times prior to the seizure of forensic samples.

Contemporaneous notes: written notes made at the time, usually in a pocket book or a CSI report form, computer log, and so on (*see also* **Original notes**).

Contempt of court: defined within the Contempt of Court Act 1981, contempt of court is aimed at protecting the integrity of the proceedings within the court that may be compromised; for example, the publication of information in a newspaper that may be read by and influence a juror, or an individual interrupting the court proceedings (*see also* **Perjury**).

Continuity: the ability to keep track and demonstrate the location of evidence throughout an enquiry from the crime scene to the court.

Control room: a range of different control rooms exist within the law enforcement arena ranging from those operated by the police and other emergency services, sometimes jointly, to control rooms operated by private organizations dedicated to surveillance using CCTV cameras. However, a police control room is usually a busy, hi-tech environment staffed by a blend of police officers and civilian specialists, who between them receive and record information through telephone calls and the emergency services airwave radio communication system. The information received is assessed; the control room staff make difficult, timely and critical decisions based on the information they have received, then resources such as individual police officers or police community support officers, air support units or armed response vehicles, and so on are deployed to deal with incidents. The control room staff will maintain contact with the staff deployed to keep up to date with how the incident is progressing, in order to ensure the health and safety of the deployed staff and so the control room know when the incident has been dealt with and the staff become available for redeployment to another incident (*see also* **Airwave, Airwave status codes** and **Phoenix**).

Conviction: when an individual is found guilty by a criminal court of the offence with which they were charged.

COP: *see* **Community-oriented policing**.

COP PLAN ID: in order to satisfy himself or herself that an arrest can be made using the Serious Organized Crime and Police Act (2005), an officer should conduct a 'test of necessity'. This may be remembered using the mnemonic COP PLAN ID. Crow et al. (2006) define this mnemonic in terms of 'is the arrest necessary?' for: **C** – Child or vulnerable witness protection;

O – Obstruction prevention; **P** – Injury prevention; **P** – Ensuring public decency; **L** – Preventing loss or damage; **A** – Queries over the correct address of the person; **N** – Queries over the correct name of the person; **I** – Investigating the offence; **D** – ensuring that the person does not disappear.

Cordons: barriers, often in the form of tape, put in place at the scene of an incident. There are usually two cordons; an inner to act as a barrier against contamination, and an outer to keep the press and general public away.

Core investigative doctrine: a doctrine developed jointly by the Association of Chief Police Officers and the National Centre for Policing Excellence in order to provide guidance on a national basis on how all criminal investigations should be conducted (Newburn et al. 2007).

Coroner: an independent member of the judiciary, usually qualified as a doctor or within the legal profession, who will hold an inquiry into any unexpected death.

Coroner's court: courts established to conduct inquiries into deaths that were violent or unnatural, sudden and cause unknown or occurred in prison (*see also* **Inquest**).

Coroner's officer: the coroner's officer usually works for the police. He or she works on behalf of the coroner investigating violent or unnatural deaths that occur within their area to assist in determining if an inquest into the death is required.

Corporate manslaughter: defined within the Corporate Manslaughter and Corporate Homicide Act 2007, the senior management of an organization may be prosecuted for a criminal offence if activities organized or managed cause, through gross health and safety failures, a death, or similarly a duty of care is breached leading to a death (*see also* **Homicide, Honour killing, Mass murder, Murder/Manslaughter, Murder manual, Serial killer** and **Spree killer**).

Corroboration: evidence from a means independent of a witness to support the witness's evidence.

COSHH: Control of Substances Hazardous to Health. These health and safety regulations focus on risk assessments and the need to prevent employees from exposure to hazardous substances, such as CS spray and aluminium fingerprint powder.

Court martial: similar to a civilian criminal Crown Court, a court martial is convened within the armed forces governed by statute and regulation to try serious offences against either civilian criminals or armed forces law by military personnel. The court is headed by a civilian judge advocate (the senior courts martial judge is appointed by the Crown as the Judge Advocate General) with a jury comprising of commissioned officers and/or warrant officers who decide on the evidence presented if the defendant is guilty or not (Judicial Communications Office 2008). Minor infringements by armed forces personnel of military law or criminal law can be dealt with summarily by the commanding officer, or alternatively the accused can request trial by a court martial (ibid.) (*see also* **Crown Court**).

Court of Appeal: divided into two courts (criminal and civil) that deals with appeals from a Crown Court or similar on matters to do with the conviction or sentence (*see also* **Magistrates Court, Criminal Cases Review Commission, Crown Court, Queens Bench Division** and **House of Lords**).

CPD: Continuous professional development; the expectation that there is a requirement to continuously update knowledge and skills (e.g. changes in the law) in order to perform a role to the best of an individual's ability.

CPIA: Criminal Procedures and Investigation Act 1996 sets out the way in which all relevant information relating to an investigation should be disclosed to the defence.

CPO: Crime prevention officer; CPOs act as a point of contact for advice and guidance within the police for both the general public and businesses who are considering adopting measures to reduce crime and the fear of crime (*see also* **Architectural liaison officer, Crime prevention through environmental design** and **Situational crime prevention**).

CPS: Crown Prosecution Service; the CPS has its foundations in the Prosecution of Offences Act 1985 (Hannibal and Mountford 2002). The CPS have responsibility for advising the police on points of law, making decisions in consultation with the police on the charges to be answered by a defendant and, as an independent organization to the police, act on behalf of the Crown taking prosecutions to a court (*see also* **Case file**).

CPT: Child protection team; a joint police and social services team focusing on the protection of children from physical or psychological abuse (*see also* **Child Protection Unit**).

Crack cocaine: an illegal drug. Crack cocaine is a base form of cocaine (cocaine hydrochloride being a salt). Unlike cocaine, it can be smoked. This is preferred by some users because the effects are felt immediately. It is found as small crystalline 'rocks' that are heated to release the vapours. The rocks contain small amounts of water, boil when the rocks are heated, producing the cracking sound that gives the drug its name (*see also* **Cocaine**).

CRB: Criminal Records Bureau; established in 2002 as an executive agency of the Home Office, CRB uses its resources to enable organizations to identify those people who may be unsuitable to work with children or vulnerable adults (CRB 2007) (*see also* **Independent Safeguarding Authority**).

CRE: Commission for Racial Equality; established as a result of the Race Relations Act 1976, the CRE aims to promote equal opportunity, eliminate racial discrimination while developing understanding and coherence between different racial and ethnic groups.

CRFP: Council for the Registration of Forensic Practitioners; established in 2000 the CRFP is an independent organization maintaining a register of currently competent forensic practitioners ranging from forensic scientist and crime scene investigators to those specializing in forensic archaeology and forensic odontology.

Crime: a crime is generally thought of as being a wrong committed against the state and society, which is usually challenged by the Crown or its agents, and punished by the state. The elements of a crime consist of the wrongful act being committed (known as the actus reus) and the state of mind of the individual or organization committing the crime (known as the mens rea).

Crime and Disorder Act 1998: a major piece of legislation that aimed to improve community safety and the youth justice system (*see also* **CDRP**).

Crime pattern analysis: using analytical tools to identify links between crimes and other related data in order to identify similarities and differences between patterns and trends; for example, 'crime hot spots' (*see also* **ANACAPA, Five × five intelligence, Intelligence, Intelligence Analyst, Intelligence Cycle, NIM** and **Watson**).

Crime prevention through environmental design: a theory for the prevention of crime, first developed by criminologists in the 1970s, which focuses on the relationships between people, use of the land and activity upon and around it. This includes solutions for preventing crime, such as ensuring there are obvious boundaries between the use of space and through housing design create the feeling of naturally occurring surveillance for residents (*see also* **Architectural Liaison Officer, CPO** and **Situational crime prevention**).

Crimesec 38: a national form completed by police officers when any controlled drugs are seized.

Crime Stoppers: a national programme launched in the late 1980s that allows the general public to anonymously report those who commit crime via a national telephone number.

Crime warden: a civilian uniformed role within law enforcement usually employed by the local authority. Crime wardens have the responsibility for conducting high-visibility patrols to help deter and thus prevent crime and anti-social behaviour along with acting as a point of accessible contact for the general public (*see also* **Neighbourhood policing** and **PCSO**).

Criminal Cases Review Commission (CCRC): established in the late 1990s as an independent body to investigate suspected miscarriages of justice. The CCRC cannot overturn convictions, but can investigate cases, of which there have been over 10 000 applications for investigation, and decide if the case should be referred to the Court of Appeal (Slapper and Kelly 2009) (*see also* **Court of Appeal, IPCC** and **Miscarriage of justice**).

Criminal damage: defined under the Criminal Damage Act 1971 as when a person destroys or damages property belonging to another person or is reckless as to whether property would be destroyed or damaged and has no lawful reason for such destruction or damage.

Criminal Defence Service: the Criminal Defence Service manages the provision of advice, guidance and representation in the police station and court for those who are under investigation and prosecution by the police but are unable to financially support such services for legal defence. This was formally known as Legal Aid (*see also* **Duty solicitor** and **Legal Aid**).

Crime scene investigator: *see* **CSE/CSI**.

Criminal Injuries Compensation Authority: the authority deals with all applications for compensation due to personal injuries sustained as a result of violent crimes committed in England, Wales and Scotland.

CRIMINT: Criminal Intelligence (*see also* **HUMINT**).

CRIMINT database: the Metropolitan Police's computerized criminal intelligence system that has been used since 1994 to record search and manage intelligence and associated information (*see also* **CRIS**).

CRIS: Crime Report Information System; a computerized IT system operated by the Metropolitan Police Service providing up-to-date information and intelligence on suspects, victims and crimes (Fido and Skinner 1999). The system can also be interrogated as to how the crimes, and all the related information, are being dealt with in order to assess performance (*see also* **CRIMINT database**).

Critical incident debriefing: to be completed as soon as is practicable after an incident, the critical incident debrief is broken down into two components. The first reflects upon the operational context, such as the response, availability of resources, and so on; the second component reviews an individual's personal experience in order to assist them in coming to terms and dealing with a traumatic event (*see also* **PTSD**).

CRO: Criminal Records Office; the first national criminal records office was established in 1913. This was dedicated to keeping up-to-date information on those convicted of offences. After regionalization and duplication of records in regional offices, the advent of the National Identification Bureau in 1980, along with the gradual advancement of technology, has reduced the need for such criminal record offices having been replaced instead with computerization (Thomas 2007) (*see also* **NIB, Phoenix** and **PNC**).

Cross-contamination: corruption of evidence taking place at either the crime scene or laboratory due to incorrect or poor packaging, inappropriate practices, such as coughing over samples, or secondary transfer, such as allowing evidence to be exchanged between the suspect and the victim's clothes when they are both transported in the same police vehicle but at different times prior to the seizing of forensic samples.

Cross-examination: when the defence counsel in a criminal case being heard in a court of law may question and challenge a witness on the evidence they have given.

Crown Court: the Crown Court operates in three tiers and has jurisdiction over all serious criminal offences, such as murder or rape. The Crown Court is headed by a judge who supervises a jury who hear the evidence presented to them by the prosecution (attempting to demonstrate the accused is guilty) and the defence (attempting to demonstrate the accused has not committed the offence) then decide on a guilty or not guilty verdict (*see also* **Court Martial, Court of Appeal, House of Lords, Magistrates Court** and **Queens Bench Division**).

CSC: crime scene coordinator; the CSC (*see also* **SSC**) is usually a senior crime scene manager, and is responsible for the strategic coordination of the forensic investigation of a number of linked crime scenes.

CSE/CSI: crime scene examiner/crime scene investigator; a CSE/CSI attends scenes of crime, victims and suspects in order to record photographically, search for and recover physical, forensic and fingerprint evidence along with intelligence. Such scenes range from those involving murder and post-mortems to volume crime and criminal damage. A CSE/CSI will also provide advice on scene protection and evidence preservation. Also known as scenes of crime officer (SOCO). First nationally recognized by the Touche Ross report (1987), the role was developed by the Association of Chief Police Officers/Forensic Science Service (1996). The 3000 CSEs/CSIs nationally can be either a police officer or civilian member of staff. They are usually employed directly by a police force or other law enforcement agency. The armed forces also have their own CSEs/CSIs. The Police Reform Act (2002) allows chief officers to designate CSEs/CSIs as investigators (*see also* **CSM** and **VCSI**).

CSM: crime scene manager; a role formalized by the Association of Chief Police Officers/Forensic Science Service (1996). A CSM is appointed at a major incident to take responsibility for the operational management for recording, searching for and recovery of physical, forensic and fingerprint evidence from a major incident, such as a murder or disaster. The management includes ensuring cordons are in the correct place, organizing the team of CSEs/CSIs, liaison and provision of advice and intelligence to the senior investigating officer and other forensic specialists (*see also* **CSE/CSI**).

CS spray: an incapacitating spray; operationally available to police officers in the UK since 1996, CS spray can be used when the officer feels that he or she is in danger, danger exists for his or her colleagues or those in the vicinity. The CS spray contains the chemicals chlorobenzylidene and methyl isobutyl ketone that are propelled from the canister by hydrogen. The effect on the person sprayed by the liquid is a temporary irritation of the eyes, nose and mouth.

CT: counter terrorism; a generic term that is often used to refer to all terrorist matters (*see also* **CTSA, CTU, NaCTSO, TAM** and **Terrorism**).

CTSA: counter terrorism security adviser; providing advice on counter terrorism matters, a CTSA's primary role is to identify potential terrorist targets, such as shopping centres, sporting arenas and pubs (NaCTSO 2007). Following the identification of potential targets the risks to these locations will be assessed and then a plan as to how to minimize the associated risk will be formulated (*see also* **CT, CTU, NaCTSO** and **Terrorism**).

CTU: Counter Terrorism Unit; several Counter Terrorism Units are located around the country operating on a regional basis to supply specialist equipment and staff seconded from forces and trained in CT activities. Staff roles include investigators, intelligence analysts and covert surveillance specialists (*see also* **CT, CTSA, NaCTSO** and **Terrorism**).

Curfew order: when an individual convicted of an offence is sentenced to reside at an approved address between certain times of the day. In order to ensure this sentence is adhered to the convicted offender will wear an electronic tag, usually around the ankle, which is monitored by a private company.

Custody assistant: a civilian role within law enforcement. Custody assistants look after the security and welfare of people in custody following their detention. This includes skilled tasks such as taking their fingerprints and DNA along with ensuring those in detention are fed (*see also* **Custody**

officer, **Custody record, Custody suite, Detention officer** and **Prisoner processing unit**).

Custody officer: an officer with the rank of sergeant or above appointed by the Chief Officer to oversee the detention of an individual under the codes of practice within the custody office (*see also* **Custody assistant, Custody record, Custody suite, Detention officer** and **Prisoner processing unit**).

Custody record: a record, usually electronic, initially completed by the custody officer, which provides the personal details of the person detained (e.g. date of birth, time and date of arrest, property in their possession), the reason why the decision was made to continue to detain the individual, along with ensuring that the individual is informed of their rights (e.g. independent legal advice). The custody record then becomes a live document that must be updated each time a decision is made about the person in custody (e.g. visits by solicitor) (*see also* **Custody officer** and **Detention officer**).

Custodial sentence: when a criminal court sentences an offender to a period of imprisonment.

Custody suite: an area within a police station, under the control of the custody officer, which is dedicated to dealing with individuals arrested and detained within police custody. The custody area usually contains the charge desk, cells, an area for taking photographs, fingerprints and DNA samples, along with rooms for the conduct of interviews (*see also* **Cell, Charge desk, Custody officer, Detention officer, Independent custody visitor** and **Prisoner processing unit**).

Cybercrime: generally used to describe the use of computer technology to commit crime (also known as hi-tech crime). Jewkes (2007) suggests that the types of crime committed by cyber criminals extend beyond traditional offences such as fraud and forgery, to include new offences, such as hacking and the creation of viruses.

D

DARS: drugs arrest referral scheme; a series of nationally funded schemes established in order to identify and assist in the treatment of offenders using drugs and subsequently break their cycle of drug use.

DAT: drug action team; partnerships established by the government in 1995 to enable local communities to work together in order to deliver the national drug strategy that focuses on reduction of the misuse of drugs and alcohol along with related problems. Drug action team partnerships include representatives from educational services, housing departments, youth offending teams and the local crime and disorder reduction partnership (CDRP).

Data Protection Act: the Data Protection Act (1998) ensures that those handling personal information comply with a set of rules and provides individuals with access to information held about them.

Date rape drugs: since the mid-1980s a number of drugs have been associated with accusations of date rape, the best known of which is Rohypnol. The use of other depressants such as GHB, ketamine and temazepam, which affect an individual's self-control and memory, have also been linked to sexual assaults (*see also* **Rohypnol**).

Daubert tests: a 1993 legal case in the USA, in *Daubert* v. *Merrell Dow Pharmaceuticals Incorporated*, the judge held that all expert scientific evidence must be relevant to the case and that any scientific evidence must be based on validated research that was reliable (Geberth 2006).

DC: detective constable; a police officer rank.

DCC: deputy chief constable; a police officer rank.

DCI: detective chief inspector; a police officer rank.

D&D: drunk and disorderly; established under the Criminal Justice Act (1967), it is an offence for a person to be disorderly while in a public place and under the influence of alcohol.

DDA: Disability Discrimination Act (2005); enhancing earlier legislation on disability discrimination, DDA aims to remove discrimination of the disabled by employers or anyone who provides a service (*see also* **Diversity**).

DE: domestic extremism; DE is any criminal act committed by an individual or group while being part of a protest or a prolonged campaign of disobedience (*see also* **NHTCU**).

DEA: drug enforcement administration; part of the US Department of Justice, the DEA was formed in 1973 with the aim of enforcing the laws of the US in relation to controlled substances across state boundaries and international borders (*see also* **SCDEA**).

Death in custody: a custody officer has a duty of care towards an individual held in police custody to take all reasonable steps to ensure that he or she is protected from harm. If an individual dies or commits suicide while in custody the death is always investigated and referred to the Independent Police Complaints Commission (*see also* **Custody officer** and **IPCC**).

Death notification: when a police officer delivers a message of the death of a family member to relatives. This type of message is a particularly difficult situation for a police officer to deal with, but as a basic principle such bad news should be delivered face to face with the relative and as soon as possible after the deceased has been identified. The death notification should be delivered in easy-to-understand and compassionate language by a pair of experienced police officers who can provide mutual support for each other.

Defence College of Policing and Guarding: a military establishment responsible for the harmonized joint initial and specialist police education and training of all Royal Navy, Army, Royal Air Force and Royal Marine personnel.

Defendant: the person charged with an offence.

DEFRA: Department for the Environment, Food and Rural Affairs; a network of agencies working under one umbrella responsible for a wide range of services, regulation and enforcement of infringements of the rules relating to farming (both on land and sea), the countryside, the environment and the rural economy along with a focus on sustainable development (DEFRA 2007).

Delta: a letter of the phonetic alphabet that is utilized to describe the letter D (*see* **Appendix 4**).

Dendrochronology: a technique for analysing tree ring growth that can be applied to a forensic examination in order to establish when trees were cut down. Such techniques have been used to match wood and as evidence leading to successful convictions for illegal logging (Wolodarsky-Franke and Lara 2005).

Department for Transport: the Department for Transport aims to provide a transport network that is suitable for the economy, environment and society as a whole (*see also* **AAIB, Driving Standards Agency, DVLA, MAIB** and **RAIB**).

Desborough Committee: a committee established in 1918 to review the police such as their organization, training, officer pay and conditions of service (Fido and Skinner 1999) (*see also* **Edmund Davies report**).

Designated investigator: *see* **Designated police staff** (*see also* **CID, IO, MIT** and **TI**).

Designated police staff: the Police Reform Act 2002 empowered chief constables to designate certain appropriate police civilian staff specialists, such as crime scene examiners/investigators, detention officers and those conducting investigations, with certain police powers enabling them, for example, to legally search for and seize items of evidence, or interview individuals in custody (*see also* **CSE/CSI** and **Detention officer**).

Designated police station: originally established under the Police and Criminal Evidence Act (1984), a designated police station is one that has been identified and designated by the chief constable as appropriate in terms of staffing and facilities for the detention of the person under arrest.

Designated sporting event: The Sports Ground and Sporting Events (Designation) Order 2005 enables, through designation, the policing of certain sporting events, such as Association, League and Premier League football matches those in the Scottish Football League and the Welsh Premier League, to include banning alcohol in the venue and on public transport to reach the venue or carrying articles, such as fireworks, for a set period before, during and after the sporting event.

Detection rates: offences detected within a department, division, force, and so on. Such detection rates are used as a measure as to performance of individuals, departments and forces.

Detention and training order: a sentence of a court of law given to a young offender aged between 12 and 17 who has a high risk of reoffending. The detention and training order is a custodial sentence with time also spent in the community under the supervision of the youth offending team (*see also* **Youth offending team**).

Detention officer: usually working with the custody suite, detention officers are responsible for the welfare of those detained and placed in their charge. Their powers are less broad than those of their custody officer colleagues (Rogers and Lewis 2007) (*see also* **Custody assistant, Custody officer, Custody record** and **Custody suite**).

Deviant behaviour: there are many suggestions as to what constitutes deviant behaviour. In fact, juvenile delinquency has been identified as far back in history as the seventeenth century. There is however general agreement that what constitutes deviance relies on the context, biography and purpose (Downes and Rock 1998) and it occurs when someone breaks what are the norms of society. However, deviant behaviour need not necessarily be a criminal act; instead, it is most likely to be considered as banned or controlled and will attract disapproval from some within the community (ibid.). Examples of deviant behaviour could be the non-wearing of a seat belt or a pupil being disruptive in a school class.

DFO: Diazafluoren-9-One; a forensic method that uses a chemical reagent to develop fingerprints on porous surfaces such as paper.

DHQ: divisional headquarters.

D&I: drunk and incapable; established under the Licensing Act (1872), it is an offence for individuals to be under the influence of alcohol and incapable of looking after themselves while in a public place, on a highway or in licensed premises.

DI: detective inspector.

DIO: drugs intelligence officer; the role of the DIO is to identify issues relating to drugs within an area and through research identify trends and problems that may be resolved through partnership working.

Diplomatic Protection Group: a department of officers, regularly armed, within the Metropolitan Police Service with responsibility for the security and protection of the foreign diplomatic community, such as the provision of static guards for embassies and/or close protection for diplomats (*see also* **Close Protection Unit**).

Disclosure: disclosure was originally defined within the Criminal Procedures and Investigation Act 1996 in order to ensure the fairness of court cases. The term 'disclosure' refers to revealing all unused material by the prosecution that does not form part of the case for the prosecution but may be pertinent to the case for the defence. The defence must be given copies or access to all this information (*see also* **Confidential, Restricted, Secret** and **Top secret**).

Discretion: in the UK police officers are servants of the Crown, which means they serve the law rather than an employer and follow the principle of 'constabulary independence'. This means that no one can tell them that they must, or must not, arrest and prosecute in any particular circumstances – they can exercise discretion on whether or not to do so. Discretion is the freedom of judgement and action, the authority to decide and choose, selecting the best course of action having recognized and considered all the alternatives. Use of discretion could be seen as favouring certain groups, so police officers must ensure that decisions that they make are fair. The courts have developed three broad legal principles to limit discretion: a prosecution should not be pursued in bad faith, the discretion exercised should be reasonable and decisions must take into consideration and apply consistent policy (Rogers and Lewis 2007; Sanders and Young 2007) (*see also* **Code of Ethics**).

Distinguishing marks: marks on an individual that may aid in their identification such as scars and tattoos (*see also* **Phoenix**).

Distraction burglary: often referred to as bogus callers, distraction burglaries are predominantly targeted at the elderly and vulnerable within society. An individual offender will call unexpectedly at a house purporting to be from the water board or gas company and distract the resident while they or another person sneaks into the home to steal items. Multi-agency task forces, including the police and council, are set up on a regular basis to conduct educational and investigative operations (e.g. Operation Strongbow) as a response to these types of offence.

Diversity: diversity means variety, and in policing terms refers to recognizing that people are different and have different needs. The guiding principle is that no one should face prejudice or discrimination simply because he or she happens to be different in some way from the majority of people. This could be because of their religious beliefs, race, gender or sexuality, age or because they have a disability. In the latter part of the twentieth century the main diversity issue for the police was race. The issue of racism within the police service was first raised by Lord Scarman in his report following the Brixton riots of 1981, where he uncovered evidence of racial prejudice within the Metropolitan Police Service and made recommendations to eliminate it. However, in 1999 the MacPherson report following the death of Stephen Lawrence found racism still to be an issue. MacPherson found that racism within the police was now much less overt, mainly 'unwitting' racism, coining the phrase 'institutional racism' (which is generally understood as stereotyping and not trying to understand those from minority communities). In recent years, changes in legislation have obliged the police to look at how they deal with sex and disability discrimination when interacting with the public, but also in how they treat their own staff. The Human Rights Act 1998 has impacted on police investigations generally, as potential adverse effects on communities or individuals must be considered (*see also* **DDA, Equal Opportunities, Institutional racism, MacPherson report** and **Scarman report**).

Dixon of Dock Green: an iconic post-war fictional beat police officer portrayed by the popular television media as the best way of policing, hence detecting and reducing crime (*see also* **Neighbourhood policing**).

DLO: drugs liaison officer; DLOs gather and disseminate intelligence from those organizations they are working in partnership with on the misuse of drugs as well as ensuring that hospitals and commercial pharmacies comply with legislation in relation to the handling and custody of controlled drugs.

DNA: deoxyribonucleic acid; a double-stranded molecule consisting of four different bases: adenine; cytosine; guanine; and thymine, the sequence of which comes together to make up our genetic code. Everyone's DNA is different, with the exception of identical twins (Jeffreys et al. 1985). In 1986 this uniqueness of DNA was first used in the investigation of crime to link the murders of two schoolgirls and the release of an individual suspected of committing the offences but proved by DNA profiling not to have been involved. This led to a mass screening in an attempt to locate the offender and the eventual identification by DNA and arrest in 1987 of Colin Pitchfork who was convicted for the crimes in 1988. In 1995 the first ever national DNA database was established in the UK. The database today holds approximately four million DNA samples of those arrested, charged, reported, cautioned or convicted of a recordable offence and several hundred thousand DNA profiles obtained from crime scenes. Both sets of profiles are searched against each other and regularly attain matches that are statistically reported as a likelihood of the match occurring, ranging from a 1 in 200 chance to a one in several million (Williams and Johnson 2008). The future developments of DNA profiling includes the possibility of sharing profiles and intelligence across international borders and the ability of the police to compare DNA profiles of those arrested with other databases held legitimately by organizations for other reasons such as those by the NHS (ibid.). Such developments raise a number of ethical questions, such as the access by the police to confidentially obtained and held records (*see also* **Buccal cells, Intimate samples, Mass screen** and **Non-intimate samples**).

DNA boost: a commercial technique developed by the Forensic Science Service that enables mixed or partial DNA crime scene stains to be enhanced, examined and interpreted.

DOA: dead on arrival.

DOB: date of birth.

Dog section: a specialist unit of law enforcement officers who are trained and work with dogs to conduct a range of duties. The majority of dogs and their police handlers can search premises for items or individuals and then if required pursue and apprehend individuals suspected of committing an offence. They are also useful for controlling crowds. Other dogs and handlers are trained to search for drugs, explosives and even bodies.

Domestic violence: often a crime hidden from public view and referred to more generically as family crime, domestic violence is when any child or adult of either gender, who are family members, receive threats of violence or behaviour, violence itself, abuse or harassment from another family member. Although reported offences of domestic violence have continued to fall since 1995 (Finney 2006), the introduction of the Domestic Violence, Crime and Victims Act 2004 has assisted both victims and witnesses of domestic violence by providing protection and support for those involved and making changes to the criminal justice system (ibid.) including allowing courts to impose appropriate restraining orders and making offences of common assault, in some circumstances, an arrestable offence.

Door ram: specially constructed battering rams used by law enforcement organizations. The door rams are made of high-grip material to prevent slipping when in use and have an impact weight of several tonnes when swung against a surface.

Doorstep bail: when an offender is given a curfew by the courts and must reside at an address during curfew hours where the police officer can call and check the conditions of the bail are being adhered to.

DPO: data protection officer; responsible for administering provisions under the Data Protection Act and dealing with enquiries for data.

DPP: director of public prosecutions; the head of the Crown Prosecution Service, the DPP has responsibility for the oversight and review of criminal cases commenced by the police across England and Wales. The DPP can also advise and guide the police on matters of criminal law (The Crown Prosecution Service 2007).

DPPO: Designated Public Places Order; the Criminal Justice and Police Act 2001 introduced the power for local authorities to ban drinking alcohol in designated areas. Such designated areas can be streets, parks or town centres. Officers can request an individual to stop drinking alcohol or confiscate alcohol in these areas.

DPS: Defence Police School, a military police training school (*see also* **Defence College of Policing and Guarding**).

Dragon lamp: A commercially produced hand-held portable searchlight used by law enforcement organizations. The lamp uses aviation standard lighting to illuminate areas over a long distance.

Driving Standards Agency: part of the Department for Transport, the DSA promotes safe driving by maintaining a database of approved instructors and provides training and assessment for drivers of vehicles ranging from motorcycles and cars to heavy goods vehicles and buses.

Drug driving: drug driving carries the same penalties as drink driving (a minimum one-year driving ban and a fine of up to £5000 or up to six months in prison). If a police officer suspects that someone's driving is impaired through the use of drugs, then a field impairment test (FIT) will be administered. This will be followed by a medical examination by a forensic medical examiner who will take a blood sample to confirm the presence of drugs. Not only illicit drugs but also prescription and over-the-counter medicines can cause impairment. Unlike with alcohol, there are no legal limits set for the levels of drugs a driver may have in their body. If drugs are detected then a prosecution will be brought on the strength of the police officer's evidence from the FIT and the forensic medical examiner's opinion of impairment (*see also* **Field impairment test** and **FME**).

Drug Intervention Programme: Drug Intervention Programmes (DIPs) were established in 2003 as a key initiative in the government's attempt to reduce crime. On arrest for certain trigger offences such as burglary, robbery or possession of class A drugs, offenders who it is believed misuse drugs are given a saliva test for opiates (heroin) and cocaine. If they are found to be positive for the use of such substances, the offender will be referred for an assessment and then placed on an individually drawn up intervention programme. The aim is to provide the offender with a route away from crime.

Drug Treatment and Testing Order: a sentence passed by the courts where the offender attends a centre to be treated for a drug addiction and then regular drug testing.

DS: detective sergeant.

DSG: Diversity Steering Group; members of the group represent the organization and provides direction on all areas of diversity and reviews progress in achieving diversity objectives.

D/Supt: detective superintendent.

DTO: divisional or district training officer.

Duty solicitor: a solicitor independent of the police or courts service who is on call to provide free legal advice and guidance either in person or via the telephone to individuals in custody (*see also* **Criminal Defence Service** and **Solicitor**).

DV: developed vetting; a comprehensive security vetting process leading to access to sensitive government, military or police material. In order to complete DV successfully, checks are made of an individual's criminal, financial and social security records, references are taken up and an interview is conducted by a specially trained vetting officer.

DVI: disaster victim identification; the identification of victims linking the details of missing persons that have been accurately recorded and collated for comparison with information on the victims collected using a variety of techniques including DNA analysis, odontology and fingerprinting.

DVLA: Driving Vehicle Licensing Agency; the DVLA's history can be traced back to the Driver Vehicle Licensing Centres established in the 1960s. The DVLA today is an executive agency of the Department of Transport. The aim of the DVLA is to assist in the maintenance of safety on the roads by maintaining databases of road users, vehicles and the collection of the vehicle excise licence (DVLA 2007).

DVU: Domestic Violence Unit; a unit of specially trained police personnel who are trained and have experience in dealing with victims of domestic violence. The units usually work closely with partner organizations, such as women's refuges and the probation service, in a multi-agency approach to dealing with and resolving issues (*see also* **Domestic violence**).

DWP: Department for Work and Pensions; working with children, those in work, those receiving pensions and the disabled, DWP aims to end child poverty, get more people into work, help people plan for retirement and assist the disabled (DWP 2007).

E

Earprints: occasionally found at crime scenes where an offender has pushed his or her ear against a surface, such as a door or window, to listen before entering the location (Pepper 2005). Earprints recovered from crime scenes can be compared and identified with a comparison print taken from a suspect. In the court case of *R* v. *Dallagher* (1996) an earprint comparison was used to convict the suspect in a murder case. However, in 2002 the conviction was quashed as there was no empirical research, and no peer review to support the conclusion of the earprint match.

Echo: a letter of the phonetic alphabet that is utilized to describe the letter E (*see* **Appendix 4**).

ECHR: European Convention on Human Rights; originally signed at the Council of Europe in 1950, the ECHR was established to provide a minimum level of protection of human rights across the states of western Europe, with the enhanced ability to redress breaches of the convention at a European court. This treaty has been further enhanced with the Human Rights Act (1998) (*see also* **European Court of Justice**).

Economic Crime Unit: a specialist police unit that deals with complex, series and serious fraud investigations (*see also* **Fraud**).

Ecstasy: an illegal drug, ecstasy is the street name for the drug methylene-dioxymethamphetamine (MDMA) that is usually in the form of a tablet. The tablets are most often white, but can be any colour, and are usually round and often slightly irregular in shape due to being hand-pressed. The tablets have many different logos, such as 'Mercedes Benz', 'doves' and 'smiley faces', with new logos being encountered regularly. The logos are designed to create brand loyalty among users, but successful logos are swiftly copied by other manufacturers hoping to cash in on their popularity, so a particular logo does not guarantee the actual contents of the pill. Users feel an overwhelming sense of euphoria, profound feelings of intimacy with and empathy towards others, described as being 'loved up'. Other effects include increased energy, heart rate, blood pressure and perspiration, and heightened perception of colour and sound. Serious complications arising from the use of ecstasy include hyperthermia (heatstroke) due to continuous dancing in a hot environment and lack of fluid intake, and also dehydration. To try to counteract these complications many clubs provide 'chill-out' areas and free water.

Edmund Davies report: a report published in 1978 leading to the reform of police conditions of service and the representation of these conditions on a national basis. The report was originally commissioned by the Home Office into the mechanisms for negotiation and the pay of police officers (*see also* **Desborough Committee, Police Federation** and **Sheehy inquiry**).

E-fit: a commercially produced IT system used across the UK and a number of other countries, which can be used by a trained and skilled operator to compile a composite electronic impression of an individual's face.

EGT: evidence gathering team; law enforcement officers especially trained to use video or stills photographic equipment to record evidence of offences being committed, such as those during the commission of public disorder.

Either way offence: one of three classifications of criminal offences. An either way offence (e.g. assault occasioning actual bodily harm, burglary or theft) is usually heard in a Magistrates court unless the magistrates, prosecution or defence feel that the case would be better dealt with within a Crown Court (Hannibal and Mountford 2002) (*see also* **Indictable offence** and **Summary offence**).

ELBOWS: a mnemonic used to remember the unwritten rules to be used when completing a pocket notebook. The rules suggest that there should be no **E**rasing of entries, **L**eaves torn out, **B**lank spaces, **O**verwriting of letters or words, **W**riting between lines, or **S**pare pages left blank (*see also* **Pocket notebook**).

ELISA: enzyme-linked immunosorbent assays; a forensic technique used to test for the presence of drugs such as amphetamines and opiates in biological samples such as blood and urine (Langford et al. 2005).

ELO: explosives liaison officer; a job role that is responsible for the correct registration, certification and licensing of explosives storage (e.g. in quarries) and provides a conduit for advice and sharing information within the force and to other law enforcement agencies in relation to the quantities, types and thefts of explosives (*see also* **EOD**).

Emergency planning officer: specially trained police officer or civilian employee of either the police or local government, an emergency planning officer has the responsibility in liaison with other agencies to anticipate and plan to deal with events, such as floods or terrorist attack, ensuring the continued safety and well-being of the general public.

Endorsable offences: a list of offences, such as speeding, which may result in a fine for the motorist and the endorsement of an individual's driving licence with a number of penalty points (*see also* **Non-endorsable offences**).

ENFSI: European Network of Forensic Science Institutes; ENSFI aims to share good practice in the development and use of forensic science across Europe.

Engine number: a unique identifying number stamped onto the engine block of all motor engines (*see also* **Chassis number, VIN** and **VRM**).

Enquiry desk officer: a civilian role within law enforcement. An enquiry desk officer would work at the front counter within the police station dealing with the general public to take reports of crimes, road traffic accidents, lost and found property (including dogs) along with checking driving documents after a request has been made by a police officer (*see also* **HORT1**).

Entomology: *see* **Forensic entomology**.

Environmental scanning: ongoing searching for and identification of political, economic, social, technical, environmental and legal developments that may impact on law enforcement (*see also* **PESTEL**).

EOD: explosives ordnance disposal; predominantly military specialists (although some civilian explosive specialists are employed in London) who are based in a number of strategic locations around the country. These specialists have technical expertise in dealing with ammunition and explosive devices and will travel to scenes of suspected explosive devices to assess and deal with what they find (*see also* **BOMB ALERT, ELO** and **IED**).

Equal Opportunities: based on a great deal of legislation including the Equal Pay Act 1970, Sex Discrimination Act 1975, Race Relations Act 1976, Disability Discrimination Act 1995 and Employment Rights Act 1996, no one should receive less favourable treatment due to their gender, marital status, race, colour, ethnic origin, nationality, religious beliefs, politics, disability, age, responsibility for dependants, socio-economic group or sexual orientation. Breaches of the legislation can be enforced through the Equality and Human Rights Commission (*see also* **Diversity**).

ESDA: electro static detection apparatus; electrical apparatus used within a laboratory to recover indented handwriting that may not be visible to the naked eye (Langford et al. 2005).

ESLA: electro static lifting apparatus; equipment operated by trained crime scene investigators that uses static electricity to recover footwear and fingerprints left in dust at crime scenes.

Establishment: number of police officers and support staff positions for which funding has been approved.

ETA: estimated time of arrival.

Ethnicity: there is no one way of defining an individual's ethnicity as this could relate to their place of birth, nationality, geographical place of origin, skin colour or religion. It is usual practice to allow an individual to self-define their believed ethnicity using a series of 16 predetermined options such as British, Chinese, Pakistani or African.

EURODAC: a European-wide computerized fingerprint identification system that contains the fingerprints of anyone who applies for asylum in the European Union and some Scandinavian countries. The database can only be used for the comparison of fingerprints taken for the purposes of asylum in order to ascertain if the individual has previously applied.

European Court of Justice: located in Luxembourg, the European Court of Justice ensures that the treaties and laws of the European Union are respected and adhered to (*see also* **ECHR**).

Europol: European police organization; based on the member states of the European Union, Europol acts as a conduit to share intelligence and information on serious and organized crime (*see also* **Interpol** and **Transnational policing**).

Evidence: all information and material, including personal evidence (e.g. statements) and physical evidence (e.g. forensic samples), which are relevant to the criminal case being investigated (*see also* **Seizure**).

Examination in chief: when the prosecutor in a criminal case being heard in a court of law will lead a witness through their evidence drawing out salient points.

Exhibit: a piece of physical evidence (as diverse as a bottle used in an assault, to a photograph of the victim, to a statement) (*see also* **Exhibit label, Exhibit log** and **Exhibit officer**).

Exhibit label: a label that is started by the person who recovers a piece of evidence and stays with the evidence throughout the enquiry to the court and eventual disposal. The exhibit label allows the evidence to be uniquely identified in the case and shows who has had the exhibit in their possession (*see also* **Exhibit, Exhibit log** and **Exhibit officer**).

Exhibit log: a register, often kept by the exhibit officer, of all exhibits recovered in relation to a particular incident (*see also* **Exhibit, Exhibit label** and **Exhibit officer**).

Exhibit officer: specially trained police officer or civilian employee who is responsible for the management, maintenance of accurate records and safekeeping of exhibits in relation to an enquiry and subsequent court proceedings. This includes each exhibit's continuity, integrity, movements and eventual disposal (*see also* **Exhibit, Exhibit label** and **Exhibit log**).

Exhumation: the removal of a body or cremated remains from the ground. A licence is required from the Home Office to exhume a body that will set out a number of conditions, such as the personnel to be involved and how the privacy is to be maintained. The appropriate permissions should also be sought if the ground is consecrated.

Expert evidence: when the evidence required by the court in order to reach a decision goes beyond that of the ordinary knowledge of those in the court, an expert witness may provide evidence. Examples of those accepted as expert witnesses by the court include fingerprint experts, forensic biologists and pathologists (Hannibal and Mountford 2002).

Extradition: a formal process for the deportation of an individual to be tried in a foreign country under that country's laws.

Eyewitness evidence: when an individual witness has observed first hand an event that is directly related to the crime being investigated (Innes 2003) although such eyewitness evidence can be subject to error such as mistaken identity (Newburn et al. 2007).

F

FACT: Federation Against Copyright Theft; established in the 1980s, the aim of FACT is to protect the film and broadcasting industry against counterfeiting and breaches of copyright, such as the pirating of DVDs. There is close liaison between FACT and the wider law enforcement community including the Metropolitan Police Film Piracy Unit (Federation Against Copyright Theft 2008) (*see also* **Metropolitan Police Film Piracy Unit**).

FAIR: forensic after incident review; a review conducted by a forensic specialist after completing the examination of an incident.

FASP: first aid skills for policing; a series of training modules designed and delivered by the National Police Improvement Agency (NPIA) targeted at teaching the skills of first aid in the context of policing.

Faulds, Henry: a nineteenth-century surgeon who suggested that the patterns forming fingerprints are persistent throughout life.

FBI: Federal Bureau of Investigation; the FBI can trace its origins back to 1908 when a group of law enforcement agents was first established. With offices across the US and in over 50 countries the FBI aims to protect the US from terrorism and the threats posed by foreign intelligence gathering while enforcing the criminal laws and justice across the US.

FBO: football banning order; originally established by the Football Spectators Act (1989), the FBO is issued by the court and prohibits the person named in the banning order from attending a regulated football match anywhere across England and Wales (*see also* **FIO** and **IFBO**).

FCP: forward control point; usually the first police vehicle to arrive at an incident will be nominated as the FCP. It is good practice for the vehicle to leave its blue lights on to indicate to all emergency responders that this is the FCP and the officer should take up interim command of the incident until the arrival and establishment of a more formal command structure. These are often in the form of specifically designed command and control vehicles from the various emergency services involved.

FDL: fingerprint development laboratory; a specially equipped laboratory in which trained personnel use sequential chemical and physical techniques to examine articles recovered from crime scenes for fingerprints and other evidence types that can then be recorded and recovered (*see also* **Superglue** and **Ninhydrin**).

FDR: firearms discharge residue; when a firearm discharges a cartridge a certain amount of the primer and propellant from the cartridge will be ejected from the weapon and deposited on the hands, face and clothing of the person firing the weapon and possibly on the victim (Warlow 2005). This minute FDR forensic evidence can be recovered from the shooter and the victim using careful forensic techniques.

Fear of crime: the fear of being a victim of crime is of concern to some individuals more than others influenced by age, gender, ethnicity, social group, locality, and so on. Such fear can lead to the individual suffering from anxiety, mistrust and alienation from the community (Liska et al. 1982). Often the perception of being a victim of crime is not founded on statistical likelihood; however, the fear itself is an issue. The British Crime Survey continually highlights people's continued fear of being a victim of crime.

Felony: a term used within the US justice system to describe a serious crime (e.g. murder) that attracts a punishment of death or imprisonment exceeding one year (*see also* **Indictable Offence, Misdemeanour** and **Summary offence**).

FEMA: Federal Emergency Management Agency; part of the Department of Homeland security in the US, FEMA aims to protect life and property across the US by training for and minimizing the effects of disaster, such as floods, earthquakes and acts of terrorism.

FEO: firearms enquiry officer; law enforcement officers who carry out personal visits to those requesting firearms, shotgun or explosives licences.

FHQ: force headquarters.

FIB: Force Intelligence Bureau; usually based within the CID, the FIB is responsible for gathering, collating and assessing intelligence from across the force, which it then disseminates. The FIB also acts as a single point of contact for other law enforcement agencies outside of the force.

Field impairment test: a field impairment test is a preliminary test carried out at the roadside when a police officer believes that a person's driving may be impaired due to drug use. The test must be carried out by an officer who is trained and qualified to do so, and includes an examination of the pupils of the eyes, a balance test, a walk and turn test, standing on one leg and touching a finger to the nose with eyes closed. The power to perform the test is contained in the Road Traffic Act 1988 (as amended by the Railways and Transport Safety Act 2003). If, after administering the test, the officer is of the opinion that the person may be under the influence of drugs, they are arrested and taken to a custody suite where they will be examined by a forensic medical examiner. If the forensic medical examiner certifies that a condition that may be due to alcohol or drugs is present, then biological samples are taken from the person for toxicological analysis (*see also* **Drug driving** and **FME**).

Fielding, John and Henry: both John and Henry Fielding were magistrates in eighteenth-century London. They published articles on cases of hideous crimes which they had dealt with and in 1750 established a group of paid constables targeted at tackling the street robbers and murders of London. The so-called 'thief takers' were based in Bow Street. After Henry died John won continued moral and financial support for the establishment of a group of constables who became known as the 'Bow Street Runners' (*see also* **Bow Street Runners, Colquhoun, Patrick, Constable** and **Peel, Robert**).

FIND: Facial Images National Database; having been successfully piloted with approaching one million digital photographic facial images taken from suspects within a custody suite, FIND is designed to enter service nationally in 2009. The recorded facial images electronically received are stored and can be retrieved remotely on a read-only basis across the UK (*see also* **Biometrics**).

Fingerprint expert: predominantly civilian staff fingerprint experts search, compare and identify fingerprints and marks against finger and palmprint collections using both Ident 1 and manual comparison. Fingerprint experts are usually registered with the Council for the Registration of Forensic Practitioners (CRFP). Trainees working towards expert status maintain and update all fingerprint forms to ensure they are processed, entered onto Ident 1 and identifications verified, along with conducting quality control of fingerprints submitted and the comparison of Ident 1 identifications.

Fingerprints: a series of raised ridges that randomly bend, turn and break forming patterns and detail which is believed to be unique to an individual. These ridges have numerous benefits to an individual, heightening his or her sense of touch, creating friction allowing us to hold objects and raising extra sweat pores. Latent fingerprints and impressions left at a crime scene can be recovered by crime scene investigators using various means (e.g. powders, intense light sources and chemicals) and then compared and identified by fingerprint experts. The first recorded use of a fingerprint identification in a court of law occurred in 1902, when a fingerprint left and recovered from the scene of a burglary in Denmark Hill, London was identified as belonging to a known offender, Harry Jackson, who was convicted by the court on this fingerprint evidence (*see also* **Arch, Biometrics, Friction ridge, Galton, Henry, Herschel, Livescan, Loop, Mass screen, Poroscopy, Tenprints** and **Whorl**).

Firearm: although amended and extended on numerous occasions a firearm is defined within the context of the Firearms Act (1968) as a lethal barrelled weapon of any description (e.g. air rifle, semi-automatic pistol or shotgun) from which any shot (e.g. from shotguns), bullet (e.g. from a rifled weapon) or other missile (e.g. a dart) can be discharged. The law in relation to firearms also includes reference to prohibited weapons (e.g. machine guns and rifle grenades); components of weapons (e.g. firing pin) and accessories (e.g. flash eliminators) (*see also* **AFO, ARV, Ballistics, NaBID** and **Tactical Firearms Unit**).

Firearms amnesty: firearms amnesties provide the opportunity for individuals to hand in legally and illegally held firearms without prosecution. The amnesties preceding the handgun ban introduced in 1997 as a result of the inquiry into the shooting of 16 children and their teacher in Dunblane, Scotland in 1996 by Thomas Hamilton led to the surrender of 142 000 handguns (Malcolm 2002).

Firearms licensing: the licensing of firearms (e.g. shotguns) to be held and used legally in the UK.

FIT: fire investigation team; trained fire fighters who have specialized and have expertise in the investigation of fire scenes to assist in determining the cause. If arson is suspected then they will work with the police to assist in the investigation.

Fit for interview: When a person detained by the police is assessed by a forensic medical examiner (FME) and psychiatrist as being of sound mind to allow a police interview to take place. As such any statements or recordings made can be used in a court of law (Gudjonsson 1995).

Fit to be detained: custody/detention officers must convince themselves that any person detained within the custody suite must be free from any injury, illness or other health problem (including those that are psychological). If in doubt the person must be checked by a health care professional engaged by the police.

FIO: football intelligence officer; a role responsible for gathering and collating information and intelligence on likely football troublemakers and consequently organizing appropriate responses (*see also* **FBO** and **IFBO**).

FIU: Financial Investigation Unit; operating under the Proceeds of Crime Act (2002), financial investigation units conduct enquiries into financial irregularities particularly in relation to drug and associated crime and can arrange the seizure of assets from convicted offenders.

Five × five intelligence: a national means of reporting and testing the reliability of intelligence received by an officer. Reviewing the source of the information and evaluating the intelligence, an officer must grade the intelligence on a scale of one to five (or A to E) ranging from a rating of one being 'always reliable/known to be true' to five being an 'untested source or known to be false' (*see also* **ANACAPA, Crime pattern analysis, Intelligence, Intelligence analyst, Intelligence cycle, NIM** and **Watson**).

FLARE: a commercially produced computerized integrated evidence management system used to track fingerprint submissions and identifications within the fingerprint bureau.

Flash search: search carried out after risk assessment due to urgency of the situation.

FLINTS: forensic linked intelligence system; a computerized system designed to search all the information routinely collected by the police service, such as command and control logs, crime reports, DNA, footwear and fingerprint evidence. The aim is to identify links between individuals, crime scenes and crime hotspots.

FLIR: forward looking infrared; equipment that provides clear thermal images through darkness, fog, and so on and can be hand-held or mounted in aircraft or boats (*see also* **ASU**).

FLO: family liaison officer; FLOs work closely with the family of a victim (usually the family of a victim of murder or other serious offence) in order to provide emotional support but also act as the conduit to share information between the family and the investigative team.

FME: forensic medical examiner; FMEs provide medical care and assessments of people in police custody, complaints against the police and police officers injured while on duty. They also attend crime scenes to pronounce life extinct and can give expert evidence in court (*see also* **Drug driving, Field impairment test, Forensic nursing** and **OPL**).

FOA: first officer attending; the FOA is the first law enforcement officer who attends the scene of an incident. The decisions the FOA makes at the incident, such as whether to request the attendance of a detective or CSI, greatly influence the future of any subsequent enquiry.

FOI: Freedom of Information Act (2000); under the FIO (2000) any information held by a public authority, such as the police, can be requested to be disclosed.

Footwear evidence: evidence that is derived from examining the soles of shoes and comparing them with impressions left at crime scenes. Comparison is made of the tread pattern and size, which gives an indication that the impression was made by the same type of shoe. It is possible to uniquely match a footwear impression from a crime scene to the shoe that made it by means of damage features found on the tread. Damage features are the little nicks and cuts that occur while the shoe is being worn; they are formed by treading on pieces of broken glass, sharp stones, and so on while the wearer is walking about. It is usually possible to find damage features on shoes if they have been worn for as little as a few hours. Because the damage features are created in a totally random manner they form a pattern that is unique to each particular shoe and can therefore be used to identify the shoe. It should be noted however that damage features are not constant. Over time they will be worn away as the sole of the shoe wears down. Also, new damage features will be created all the time. It is therefore important that suspect shoes should be seized for comparison at the earliest opportunity to enable accurate comparisons to be made. The Serious Organized Crime and Police Act (2005) gives the power to take impressions from the footwear of people who have been arrested, for the purpose of performing a speculative search against impressions taken from crime scenes. The person must be told that this has been done, and the custody record endorsed to this effect. The impressions are normally taken using an inkless printing kit such as Printscan. Computer database systems (e.g. Shoefit and SICAR) have been developed to facilitate storage and comparison of footwear impressions from prisoners' footwear and those from crime scenes (*see also* **Printscan, Shoefit** and **SICAR**).

Force identification code: each police force has a unique number (e.g. Durham Constabulary 11 and West Mercia 22) that is utilized in administrative processes to identify the particular force.

Force Standing Order: a regulation put in place by the force to which all must adhere.

Forensic anthropology: the forensic scientific study of physical skeletal remains recovered using forensic archaeology. Such an examination can swiftly determine if remains are animal or human.

Forensic archaelogy: the forensic scientific study of the search for and recovery of buried remains.

Forensic biology: the forensic scientific study of biological and other body fluids, ranging from DNA profiling to the examination of blood spatter, and their uses in the investigation of crime.

Forensic chemistry: using the analytical techniques and equipment of chemistry to examine evidence such as glass, paint and fibres in relation to the investigation of crime.

Forensic computing: the forensic study of computer hardware, software and other digital records, such as mobile telephones and digital cameras.

Forensic entomology: the forensic study of insects and their impact on the body of a deceased in order to assist in the establishment of the time and location of death.

Forensic firearms: the forensic study of firearms, bullets, cartridges and other projectiles used as weapons. Firearms specialists can compare evidence such as bullets recovered from a crime scene to ascertain from which firearm it was discharged (*see also* **Ballistics**).

Forensic investigator: *see* **CSE/CSI**.

Forensic linguistics: the forensic study of language within a legal context.

Forensic nursing: forensic nursing is a speciality that includes providing care to victims of crime, collecting evidence and providing health care within the prison and police custody systems. The main types of forensic nurse are: the sexual assault nurse examiner (SANE) who examines victims of sexual assault and collects forensic evidence that may identify an offender; and the custody nurse who provides therapeutic care to and may undertake clinical examination of alleged perpetrators of crime. They provide evidence of fact and also nursing opinion to the court. Another sub-specialty is that of the forensic mental health nurse who cares for the mentally disordered offenders while they are in custody (*see also* **FME** and **SARC**).

Forensic odontologist: the forensic scientific study and identification of the physiological construction and anatomy of teeth. This is usually achieved by comparing pre-mortem and post-mortem dental records. Odontologists can also compare bite marks on victims with impressions of the teeth from suspects.

Forensic psychology: usually working in clinical practice, forensic psychologists use their expertise to assist in evaluating the psychological state of an individual. Some psychologists can act as profilers providing guidance to an investigative team on likely characteristics of an unknown offender.

Forensic science: the application of science to the law.

Forensic science regulator: an individual appointed by the Home Office to ensure that the forensic science services provided by a range of agencies across the criminal justice system adhere to the high-quality standards expected from forensic science.

Forensic toxicology: the forensic study of poisons and other toxic substances that may have been used within the commission of a crime.

Foundation degree: a Foundation degree is a nationally recognized educational and training qualification. The two-year Foundation degree programme of study was initially established by the Higher Education Funding Council and the Department for Education and Skills in 2001/2002. The aim is to provide learners with technical skills, academic knowledge and transferable skills that are relevant to their employment, which also meet the needs of their employer and provides access for employees to educational study. A number of police forces as part of the Initial Police Learning and Development Programme (IPLDP) have opted for Foundation degrees as the means of educating and training their probationary police officers (*see also* **IPLDP** and **NVQ**).

Found property: property found by individuals that does not belong to them.

Foxtrot: a letter of the phonetic alphabet that is utilized to describe the letter F (*see* **Appendix 4**).

FP: Fingerprint (*see* **Fingerprints**).

FPN: fixed penalty notice; these can be issued for certain offences, traditionally those involving motoring, but this has recently been extended to include other anti-social behaviour (*see also* **Central ticket office**).

Fraud: defined within the Fraud Act 2006, an offence of fraud can be committed when someone, using deception, makes a false representation, fails to disclose information or abuses their position dishonestly in order to gain an advantage, which could be financial, to obtain goods or services (e.g. using someone's bank card or identity without their knowledge) (*see also* **Economic Crime Unit**).

Friction ridge: the ridges on the fingers, hands and palms of feet, features of which are used for the purposes of identification (*see also* **Fingerprints**).

FSA: Forensic Science Agency (of Northern Ireland); provides the complete range of forensic science techniques to the region, ranging from DNA profiling to analysing for explosives, from its laboratories in Belfast (*see also* **PSNI**).

FSS: forensic science service; one of the first and largest providers of forensic investigative techniques to law enforcement including DNA analysis, toxicology, firearms and hi-tech crime (*see also* **LGC forensics**).

FTE: full-time equivalent; a proportion of a nominal full-time officer. FTE is used for calculating officer establishment numbers, salaries, leave entitlement, and so on.

FY: financial year; the financial year runs from 1 April until the following 31 March for accounting purposes.

G

Galton, Francis: an eminent nineteenth-century scientist with an interest in a number of disciplines including anthropology, exploration, human heredity, meteorology and statistics. With an interest in the uses of anthropometry, Galton conducted substantial research into fingerprint patterns and their uses in the identification of criminals (*see also* **Anthropometry** and **Fingerprints**).

Gang: although difficult to define, a gang is generally seen to be a group of individuals who come together with a structure, solidarity and a sense of belonging in order to commit a criminal act.

Gay Police Association: an association working towards equal opportunities for gay and lesbian employees.

GBH: grievous bodily harm (*see* **Wounding**).

GCHQ: Government Communications Headquarters; a government department, GCHQ uses state-of-the-art technology to obtain information and intelligence by intercepting and 'listening' to signals transmissions around the world. The department also has responsibility for assuring the safety and security of a range of government information and communication technology systems.

GCMS: gas chromatography mass spectrometry; forensic chemistry equipment used to separate and then analyse mixtures of substances.

Gelatine lifts: a fingerprint lifting tape covered in a thin layer of gelatine that allows fingerprints to be recovered when developed using granular powders or from some rough surfaces.

Genesis database: a secure police database of experts and those with experience of dealing with evidence and incidents as diverse as the laboratory examination of wood samples (*see* **Dendrochronology**) to the profiling of an offender. The database is held and maintained by the National Crime and Operations Faculty (*see also* **NCOF**).

GENIE: a commercially produced computerized integrated evidence management system used to track DNA samples.

George Cross: a silver medal in the shape of a cross with a blue ribbon. Introduced during the 1940s this is the highest medal that can be awarded to non-military personnel for outstanding acts of bravery. This may be worn on a police officer's uniform (*see also* **QGM** and **QPM**).

GHB: gamma hydroxybutyrate is a synthetic drug. Manufactured as an anaesthetic. It is a colourless and odourless liquid easily mistaken for water except for its slightly salty taste. It has been abused by body builders because it is said to promote the type of sleep that is best for muscle development. It has also appeared on the club scene, where it is sold in small plastic bottles, because in low doses it lowers inhibitions and increases libido. Higher doses cause sleepiness and confusion, so it has also been used as a date rape drug. Very high doses can lead to coma, respiratory collapse and death.

GIS: geographic information system; an IT system used for the analysis and predictions of crime patterns and trends.

GMP: Greater Manchester Police (*see* **Appendix 1**).

GMT: Greenwich Mean Time; worldwide standard time based on the prime meridian running through Greenwich.

Gold commander: the commander responsible for the executive-based strategic decisions in relation to a major incident. The gold commander has overall responsibility for the strategic management and liaison with his or her counterpart in each of the emergency services involved with the incident. Also called strategic commander (*see also* **Bronze commander, Golden hour** and **Silver commander**).

Golden hour: referring to the first 60 minutes after an incident, the golden hour is the most important for the survival of the injured and the identification of evidence (*see also* **Bronze commander, Silver commander** and **Gold commander**).

Golf: a letter of the phonetic alphabet that is utilized to describe the letter G (*see* **Appendix 4**).

GOWISELY: a mnemonic to assist officers in remembering the information that should be given to a person experiencing a stop and search. **G**rounds of the search, **O**bjective of the search, **W**arrant card shown if not in uniform, **I**dentity of the officer, **S**tation where the officer is based, **E**ntitlement to a copy of the search documentation, **L**egal powers used for the stop and search, **Y**ou have been detained for the purposes of the search (*see also* **Stop and search**).

GPS: global positioning system; devices that can be hand-held or attached to vehicles to allow their location to be accurately plotted by interpreting signals transmitted from a series of satellites.

GRIM: glass refractive index measurement; a specialist piece of laboratory equipment used by forensic scientists to measure and then compare the refractive index of samples of glass recovered from crime scenes.

Grooming: generally held to be when a child under 16, who has been met via the internet, has a meeting arranged with the groomer or another person with the intention of committing a sexual act.

GSI: government-secure intranet; a secure network for the transmission of electronic communications within law enforcement organizations and other partners with similar GSI network capability such as the National Health Service and local government.

GSR: gun shot residue (*see* **FDR**).

H

Handcuffs: a means of restraining an individual who may become violent or attempt to escape. 'Quick cuffs' are handcuffs that have the chain linking the cuff bracelets replaced by a rigid bar which allows more control of the person wearing the handcuffs.

Hate crime: a crime where the offender has a prejudice against a particular group of people, such as ethnic minorities or refugees, which, in turn, influences his or her choice of victim. The offender believes there is some association between the victim and the particular group but this may not be the case. As such anyone could be a victim of hate crime (ACPO 2000).

HAZCHEM: hazardous chemicals such as acids, radioactive materials, toxins and volatile chemicals that are transported by road, rail and air (*see also* **CHEMET** and **COSHH**).

HE: high explosives; military, commercial and home manufactured explosives are all powerful and usually require a strong force to initiate an explosion.

Health and safety: the Health and Safety at Work Act (1974) provides an overview of health and safety regulations within the workplace. The act focuses on the allocation of duty of care. Everyone is responsible for their own health and safety and the health and safety of those around them. This ranges from the responsibility of employers towards their employees, through to the responsibilities of workers and those they come into contact with. Manual handling operations deal with the safety issues related to safe lifting and moving of every kind of load (*see also* **Biohazard** and **HSE**).

Hearsay: evidence provided in an oral or written form that is not a first-hand account of what has occurred.

Henry, Edward: led a team in the late nineteenth-century India that devised a system to record and compare fingerprints. In 1901 Edward Henry established the first fingerprint bureau in the UK at Scotland Yard (*see also* **Fingerprints**).

Heroin: an illegal drug usually found in the form of a brown to white powder depending on its purity. It is an opiate derived from the opium poppy, and is synthesized from morphine. Heroin can be inhaled, or smoked by placing it on a piece of aluminium foil, heating the underside of the foil with a lighter and inhaling the resultant fumes – known as 'chasing the dragon' or injected. Heroin is not readily soluble in water, so it is usually mixed with citric acid powder or lemon juice to make an acidic solution in which it will dissolve. Heroin is used therapeutically as a painkiller, and is abused as a recreational drug because of the intense feeling of euphoria and well-being it induces. Heroin is highly addictive, ceasing to take the drug after as little as three days' usage can lead to withdrawal symptoms of nausea, vomiting, shivering and sweating (cold turkey). Users quickly build up a tolerance to the drug, meaning that ever larger doses are required to produce the same effect. Street heroin is usually mixed (cut) with other substances such as scouring powder, milk powder or talc to increase its bulk and therefore the number of deals (portions) that can be obtained from it. This cutting is usually done at each stage in the supply chain, so the strength of the drug bought on the street is dictated by how many hands it has passed through before reaching the street dealer.

Herschel, William: a nineteenth-century civil servant working in India who suggested that recording fingerprints could be used as a means to prevent locals defrauding the government (*see also* **Fingerprints**).

Highways Agency: an executive agency of the Department of Transport responsible for managing and improving the strategic road network across England. The Traffic Management Act 2004 gave the new traffic officers employed by the Highways Agency the necessary powers to carry out tasks, such as closing roads and lanes, previously conducted by the police (Highways Agency 2007).

Hip flask defence: the suggestion that someone who has been detained for any offence related to alcohol and driving has had the opportunity to consume alcohol between the time they were stopped by the police and the time a breath test was taken (*see also* **Intoximeter** and **OPL**).

HMCS: Her Majesty's Courts Service; an executive agency of the Ministry of Justice that has responsibility for the delivery of an effective and efficient courts system (HMCS 2007) (*see also* **Court of Appeal, Crown Court, House of Lords, Magistrates Court** and **Queens Bench Division**).

HMG: Her Majesty's Government.

HMIC: Her Majesty's Inspectorate of Constabulary; an independent body that examines the effectiveness of policing across England, Wales and Northern Ireland.

HMP: Her Majesty's Prison.

HM Revenue and Customs: Established in 2005, HM Revenue and Customs is predominantly concerned with collecting taxes from the right people at the right time.

HMSO: Her Majesty's Stationery Office; within the Office of Public Sector Information, HMSO is responsible for the publication of legislation and related government information.

HOLAB: Home Office laboratory; an outdated term used to describe a forensic laboratory used by the police service.

HOLMES II: Home Office Large Major Enquiry System; a computerized system used by all 43 police forces across England and Wales (Adderley and Musgrove 2001) that records, analyses and links data from the vast number of descriptions, documents, samples and information, which is collected as part of a major incident. The HOLMES computer system was originally developed in the early 1980s predominantly as a result of the Byford report into the investigation of the 13 murders and 7 attempted murders committed by the 'Yorkshire Ripper' during the late 1970s, later known to be Peter Sutcliffe. During the investigation vast amounts of information was collected including over 30 000 statements taken by the police. However, the information contained within documents (which included references to Peter Sutcliffe) were never linked (*see also* **Byford report, Indexer** and **Major incident room**).

Home Office: a large government department that takes the national lead on protecting the general public from crime and related issues by aiming to make people feel safe within their homes, reducing crime, providing visible and accountable policing, protect the community from terrorist acts, secure international borders, protect people's identity and provide the delivery of justice (Home Office 2007a). The Home Office has broad administrative responsibility for the 43 so-called 'Home Office Police Forces' across England and Wales (*see* **Appendix 1**).

Home Office Counting Rules: a set of nationally recognized rules for recording and classifying incidents and criminal (notifiable) offences that occur across the police forces in England and Wales (*see also* **National Crime Recording Standard** and **Offences brought to justice**).

Homicide: the unlawful killing of one human being by another human being. Homicides are graded by the police from A to C where grade A is a murder that creates 'great public concern' (e.g. multiple victims) to grade C where the offender is believed to be known to the police. The aim of the grading is not to attach any moral judgement to the severity of the crime but to ensure that adequate and appropriate resources are allocated to the investigation (Innes 2003). Despite the efforts of the police investigative teams approximately 10 per cent of the 700 or so homicides that occur annually in England and Wales remain undetected by the police (ibid.) (*see also* **Corporate manslaughter, Honour killing, Mass murder, Murder/Manslaughter, Murder manual, Serial killer** and **Spree killer**).

Homicide and major enquiry team: a West Yorkshire police team established in 2006 to investigate serious crime. The team came to the fore with the successful 'cold case' re-investigation of the hoax Yorkshire Ripper letters and tapes.

Homophobic incident: a homophobic incident is any occurrence that any person, such as the victim or a witness, believes to be focused on lesbian, gay, bisexual or transgender individuals or those perceived to fall into these groups (ACPO 2000).

Honour killing: an honour killing is a label used to relate to a murder committed to punish a person (most often female) whom the victim's family or community believe has brought shame on the family. The murder is normally committed by members of the victim's family, or their agents. Honour killings usually occur where a woman has refused a forced marriage, sought a divorce, been sexually abused or committed adultery. Males are also sometimes killed for refusing a forced marriage or by the family of a 'dishonoured' female. They are most common in Muslim, Hindu and Sikh communities, but have also occurred in some Druze and Christian communities in Arab countries. Although accurate data is hard to collect, research suggests that a large number of domestic murders occur around the world which could be labelled as 'honour killings' (Faqir 2001) (*see also* **Homicide** and **Murder/Manslaughter**).

HORT1: Home Office Road Traffic Form 1; can be issued by a police officer or special constable to the driver of a vehicle in order for the driver to produce documents, such as an insurance certificate, at a police station for checking within a set period of time (*see* **Enquiry desk officer**).

Hostage negotiator: a hostage negotiator is responsible for dealing with hostage- and suicide-related incidents through negotiations. They may be deployed where negotiations are necessary to ensure the safety of a person and are usually police officers of at least the rank of inspector. They undergo specialist training and perform this role as a secondary duty and on a voluntary basis.

Hotel: a letter of the phonetic alphabet that is utilized to describe the letter H (*see* **Appendix 4**).

Hotspots: areas identified by intelligence analysts using analytical tools as being increased and high concentrations of particular types of crime and are thus likely for repeat offences (*see also* **Cold spots** and **Intelligence analyst**).

House of Lords: the highest court in the land. In exceptional cases the House of Lords may hear appeals from a lower court (HMCS 2007) (*see also* **Court of Appeal, Crown Court, Magistrates Court** and **Queens Bench Division**).

HPDS: high potential development scheme; an accelerated promotion scheme for graduates, aimed at the development of potential into realizations of leadership and management for the police service (*see also* **Accelerated promotion scheme**).

HPLC: high performance liquid chromotography; forensic chemistry equipment used to separate and then analyse mixtures of substances.

HQ: Headquarters.

HR: Human Resources; a police department responsible for managing people, and the related issues such as recruitment and pay, within the organization.

HSE: Health and Safety Executive; HSE aim to ensure the safety of people in the workplace by minimizing any risks of injury or death. HSE are also responsible for investigating and prosecuting breaches of health and safety law (HSE 2007) (*see also* **Health and Safety** and **RIDDOR**).

Human rights: the Human Rights Act (1998) brought the European Convention on Human Rights (1948) into the law of the UK (Merritt 2007). The Act prohibits torture, slavery and inhuman treatment, provides the right for a fair trial and the right for respect of private and family life.

HUMINT: Human Intelligence; the gathering and collation of intelligence from individuals (*see also* **CHIS** and **CRIMINT**).

Hydra-Minerva: Operated by the National Centre for Applied Learning Technologies, Hydra-Minerva is an IT-based virtual suite allowing students to train and practise command and control simulations.

Hydrofluoric acid: a strong acid that can be found in burnt-out vehicles. If hydrofluoric acid comes into contact with the skin it can be absorbed and attack the calcium in the bones (Weissman 2002).

Hyoid bone: a small butterfly-shaped bone in the neck of an individual that often breaks if a person is strangled (*see also* **PM**).

Hypostasis: dark lines that appear on a body where the blood pools and fixes after death (*see also* **PM**).

Hypoxia: the reduction of oxygen reaching the brain which, if not alleviated, can lead to death (*see also* **Asphyxia**).

I

IAG: independent advisory group; an independent group established by the police for consultation within an area to advise on the needs of policing the community in order to develop the trust of those within the community. IAG members usually have specialist knowledge and/or experience of under-represented or minority groups (*see also* **MacPherson report**).

IAI: International Association for Identification; an association based in the US but representing the needs of those working within the forensic professions in over 70 countries (Pepper 2005).

IAS: Immigration Advisory Service; a UK-based charity that provides advice and guidance on immigration and the associated law.

ICIDP: Initial Criminal Investigators Development Programme; a nationally recognized investigator's (detective) course that includes training to a level 2

PIP standard for the investigation of both volume crimes, serious crimes and investigative interviewing to the level 2 standard (*see also* **CID, PIP** and **TI**).

ICF: Integrated Competency Framework; developed by Skills for Justice, the ICF details the core competencies that should be achieved by any police officer at any level in order to effectively perform his or her role.

ICIS: Integrated Custody Information System, a means of recording on a computer-based system details and movements of those held in custody.

ICP: Incident control point; a command and control facility (often in a vehicle) established at the location of an incident.

ID: identification.

Ident 1: A computerized identification system first used in 2004 and predominantly associated with fingerprint comparison and identification. With the ability to hold over eight million sets of fingerprints and two million marks recovered from crime scenes (McCartney 2006), Ident 1 supersedes NAFIS, supports Livescan and has been expanded to include the storage and identification of palmprints. Future expansion may also include footwear and other identification databases (*see also* **Livescan** and **NAFIS**).

Identification parade: a process where a number of individuals who have similar physical characteristics (e.g. height, hair colour, etc.) to the suspect in a case stand in a line with the suspect. Witnesses then view the line-up in an attempt to visually identify the person who they saw committing the offence. This process has been largely superseded by the introduction of the VIPER system (*see also* **VIPER**).

Identity theft: when personal information is taken by another individual and used fraudulently; for example, to open a bank account, obtain a loan or a passport. These types of occurrence continue to increase across the UK with the number of reported victims between January and September 2007 exceeding 52 000 (Furnell 2007).

IED: improvised explosive device; a number of items that were never designed to be put together, but when they are create a device which can explode and cause damage, injury or death (Thurman 2006) (*see also* **EOD**).

IFBO: international football banning order; introduced as part of the Football (Offences and Disorder) Act 1999, IFBOs restrict the movement of individuals attempting to attend football matches outside of England and Wales (*see also* **FBO** and **FIO**).

IIMARCH: Information, Intention, Method, Administration, Risk Assessment, Communication and Human Rights; a mnemonic used to assist in the planning, briefing and debriefing of a policing operation.

IIP: Investors In People; a quality mark that is used to demonstrate how the organization has been improved by investing in its employees.

ILET: international liaison and enquiry team.

Impact Nominal Index: a Home Office-run national index allowing forces across England and Wales to share information and intelligence on individuals of interest.

IMS: information management system.

In camera: when a court hearing is held in private (*see* **Open court**).

Incident data recorder: a number of police vehicles are fitted with incident data recorders (sometimes referred to as IDR) that will record data on the vehicle (e.g. speed) for a short period of time before and after any collision (NCPE 2006).

Independent custody visitor: people appointed from the local community who can visit police station custody suites unannounced to check on the general welfare of those in custody (*see also* **Custody suite**).

Independent patrol: when a probationary police officer reaches a stage of competency when they are deemed to be appropriate to deal with incidents on their own and as such become a deployable independent resource for policing (*see also* **PACS, Probationer police officer, Reflective diary** and **SOLAP**).

Independent Police Complaints Commission (IPCC): starting its work in 2004 the IPCC investigates, either directly or by proxy, serious complaints against the police (*see also* **Accountability, Criminal Cases Review Commission, Death in custody** and **Miscarriage of justice**).

Independent Safeguarding Authority (ISA): established as a result of the Bichard Inquiry into the murders in Soham in 2002 of the children Jessica Chapman and Holly Wells. ISA is an independent agency that works in partnership with the CRB to assess the suitability of any individual who works, or volunteers to work, with children or vulnerable adults (*see also* **Bichard** and **CRB**).

Indexer: a specialist administrative role within a major incident room usually associated with the maintenance of accurate records and interrogation of all information that may be relevant to the investigation. This is achieved utilizing the HOLMES II computer system. Working within a team, an Indexer would usually register all the incoming documents (e.g. statements or intelligence reports), index the contents of the documents (e.g. the linking names or locations appearing in statements) and then raise clear actions to be completed by investigating officers (e.g. visiting a particular individual) (*see also* **HOLMES II** and **Major incident room**).

India: a letter of the phonetic alphabet that is utilized to describe the letter I (*see* **Appendix 4**).

Indictable offence: one of three classifications of criminal offences. A serious indictable offence (e.g. murder, manslaughter or rape) must be heard, on indictment, before a jury in a Crown Court (Hannibal and Mountford 2002), although an earlier initial hearing will be held in a magistrates court to decide if bail is appropriate (*see also* **Either way offence** and **Summary offence**).

Infanticide: the murder of a young infant.

INFOSEC: Information Security; as threats exist to the illegal intrusion of IT, such as the hacking of IT systems or the eavesdropping on mobile telephone communications, information security attempts through a number of methods to ensure that systems and the associated information are kept confidential, their integrity is maintained, they are available, legitimately used and users are accountable for their actions (Crampton et al. 2006).

Injunction: an order created by the criminal court requiring an offender to do something or not to do something.

Inquest: held by a Coroner, an inquest is held to determine where, when and how an individual died and in some cases to establish the identity of an individual (*see also* **Coroner's court**).

Insp: inspector.

Institutional racism: defined with the 1999 inquiry into the murder of Stephen Lawrence in 1993, institutional racism is said to exist in an organization when it fails to provide the appropriate professional services to individuals because of their colour, culture or ethnic origin, it can be seen or detected in the processes, attitudes and behaviours that exist within the organization which, in turn, amount to discrimination and thus disadvantage people from ethnic minority groups. The institutional racism persists due to the failure of the organization to recognize and acknowledge its existence and hence address it (MacPherson 2007) (*see also* **Diversity, McPherson Report** and **Scarman Report**).

Integrity: ensuring that continuity of sealed samples is maintained.

Intelligence: information collected from a variety of sources that can be analysed, processed and disseminated to the appropriate people within the organization (*see also* **ANACAPA, Crime pattern analysis, Five** × **five**

intelligence, **Intelligence analyst, Intelligence cycle, Intelligence-led policing, NIM** and **Watson**).

Intelligence analyst: a civilian role within law enforcement. An intelligence analyst collates and analyses information using IT from crime reports, witness statements and intelligence reports, then provides analytical support to operational policing by supplying timely intelligence products that will assist in the prevention and detection of crime (*see also* **ANACAPA, Cold spots, Crime pattern analysis, Five** × **five intelligence, Hotspots, Intelligence, Intelligence cycle, NIM** and **Watson**).

Intelligence cycle: a number of stages through which intelligence is defined as such collated, analysed, disseminated, feedback and reviewed (Ratcliffe 2004) (*see also* **ANACAPA, Crime pattern analysis, Five** × **five intelligence, Intelligence, Intelligence analyst, NIM** and **Watson**).

Intelligence-led policing: a method of policing focused on gathering and processing intelligence in order to identify targets to assist in the reduction of incidents (*see also* **ANACAPA, Cold spots, Crime pattern analysis, Five** × **five intelligence, Hotspots, Intelligence, Intelligence analyst, Intelligence cycle, NIM** and **Watson**).

International Criminal Court: established in The Hague during 2002, the International Criminal Court (ICC) was set up to deal with perpetrators of war crimes and/or crimes against humanity.

Interpol: International Criminal Police Organization; a policing organization established in 1956 in Lyon in order to share information and intelligence across all the member countries (*see also* **Europol** and **Transnational policing**).

Interview: a method for gathering information from victims, witnesses and suspects. The standard PEACE pneumonic model is used for this process (*see also* **Cognitive interview** and **PEACE**).

Intimate samples: under the Police and Criminal Evidence Act (1984) and the Criminal Justice and Police Act (2001), intimate samples, with the exception of urine, must be taken by a medical professional (e.g. general practitioner or nurse) from a person with their consent. Samples include blood and dental impression (*see also* **Intimate search** and **Non-intimate samples**).

Intimate search: defined within the Police and Criminal Evidence Act (1984), an intimate search is when a physical search is conducted of the orifices of an individual's body. An intimate search does not include searching the mouth (*see also* **Intimate samples, Search** and **Non-intimate samples**).

Intoximeter: equipment approved by the Home Office that is used by specially trained officers to analyse specimens of breath to determine the concentration of alcohol within the breath from those individuals detained for offences related to alcohol and driving. The range of approved intoximeters (e.g. those produced by Lion, Alcosensor and Camic) must be well maintained and regularly calibrated (*see also* **Hip flask defence** and **OPL**).

IO: investigating officer; the law enforcement officer responsible for progressing an investigation until its conclusion (*see also* **CID, Designated investigator, MIT, OIC** and **TI**).

IoM: Isle of Man.

IP: injured party; the individual who is the victim of the crime.

IPA: International Police Association; a voluntary organization that through friendships shares a sense of community and professional practice between both serving and retired police officers.

IPCC: See **Independent Police Complaints Commission**.

IPLDP: Initial Police Learning and Development Programme; following a national review of the training provided to probationary police officers during the early part of the twenty-first century, the government highlighted the need for the modernization of probationer training in order to cater for the needs of modern policing and the local communities which they serve. The IPLDP represents changes to the design and delivery of the training and education of newly recruited police officers with each police force across England and Wales taking the responsibility for the local delivery of the training and education of their officers (*see also* **Community placement, Foundation degree, NVQ, Probationer police officer, PTP, Reflective diary** and **SOLAP**).

IPP sentence: Imprisonment for Public Protection sentence; introduced as part of the Criminal Justice Act (2003), an IPP sentence is a minimum term of imprisonment imposed by a criminal court that must be served by the offender prior to any hearing for parole. After release the offender must remain on licence for a number of years.

IPR: Intellectual property rights; something that has been designed or conceptualized by an individual which provides ownership of the idea (Adamo et al. 2008).

ISO: International Standards Organization; this provides recognition and accreditation of demonstrable good working practices such as ISO 9000 demonstrating good quality management and ISO 14001 demonstrating good environmental management.

J

JBB: Joint Branch Board; an element of the Police Federation where each police force has representatives from their force at the ranks of constable, sergeant and inspector, who together ensure that the needs of police officers within that particular force area are represented within the all-encompassing Federation (*see also* **Police Federation**).

Jeffreys, Alec: A twentieth-century scientist who first suggested in 1985 that DNA was specific to an individual and could be used as a means of identification (Jeffreys et al. 1985). In 1986 Jeffreys' suggestion was put to the test in an investigation into the murder of two schoolchildren three years apart. The success of DNA profiling led to the eventual conviction of Colin Pitchfork (*see also* **DNA**).

JIC: Joint Intelligence Committee; consisting of senior members of a range of government departments including the Ministry of Defence, Treasury, Foreign and Commonwealth Office, MI5 and MI6. JIC is a means by which intelligence assessments for immediate and longer-term consideration impacting on the UK are shared between departments (HM Government 2007).

JLO: juvenile liaison officer; a police officer role that is focused on young people (those under 17 years old) within a community. The JLO will attempt to resolve misdemeanours without recourse to the courts system; this can be achieved through partnership working with the local educational providers, and so on and/or a series of warnings that can be given by the police officer to the juvenile.

Job-related fitness test: fitness tests given to potential and new police recruits, and in some police forces special constables and police community support officers, which they must pass. The tests involve a shuttle run between two lines 15 metres apart while keeping pace with a series of bleeps that gradually increase in speed, plus a dynamic strength push and pull test using a Dyno machine. Each recruit must complete five seated chest pushes and five seated back pulls achieving specific weights (*see also* **PIRT** and **SEARCH assessment**).

JP: Justice of the Peace; with their routes traced back to fourteenth-century England, JPs (or magistrates) are appointed by the Lord Chancellor to conduct judicial proceedings within a particular geographical area on behalf of the Crown. They represent the local community, are not usually legally qualified but have gone through a training programme and are not paid (other than expenses) for their part-time role within the criminal justice system (*see also* **Judge** and **Magistrates Court**).

JTAC: Joint Terrorism Analysis Centre; a government department created in 2002 to analyse and disseminate intelligence related to terrorism (Henry and Smith 2007). JTAC sets the threat levels issued that range from a 'low threat' (an attack is unlikely) through a range to a 'critical threat' (an attack is imminent) (*see also* **Terrorism**).

Judge: there are three types of judge: High Court judge, circuit judge and recorder, all of whom can preside over a Crown Court. The judge, who in effect heads the court, is responsible for supervising the swearing in of the jury, ensuring the court is run fairly while advising on matters of law, summing up the evidence presented to the jury and if the defendant is found guilty by the jury, passing sentence (*see also* **JP**).

Judgment: the decision of the court in a particular case.

Judicial review: a procedure in administrative law that allows the courts to supervise the use of public power. Judicial reviews are conducted by judges on decisions made by public bodies to determine if the ruling made was lawful.

Juliet: a letter of the phonetic alphabet that is utilized to describe the letter J (*see* **Appendix 4**).

Jury: individuals selected at random from the electoral register (usually 12) brought together to hear a criminal trial, and occasionally a coroner's inquest, and then decide on a verdict.

Juvenile offender: a young person between the ages of 10 and 17 who has committed an offence.

K

Ketamine: ketamine hydrochloride is a drug that comes in varying forms including tablets and powder. It is used in human and veterinary medicine to induce and maintain anaesthesia. When used the drug causes hallucinations including out-of-body experiences, euphoria and lethargy. It is often combined with other drugs to enhance their effects.

Kilo: a letter of the phonetic alphabet that is utilized to describe the letter K (*see* **Appendix 4**).

KM: Kastle Meyer Reagent; one of a number of commercially manufactured presumptive blood testing kits that allow appropriately trained personnel; usually CSIs or forensic scientists, to swiftly distinguish between apparent blood and other red stains such as varnish or coffee stains (Pepper 2005) (*see also* **LMG**).

KPI: Key Performance Indicator; a measurement used to assess performance, such as the number of arrests (*see also* **Offences brought to justice**).

L

Laming Inquiry: an inquiry in 2003 chaired by Lord Laming into the death of the child Victoria Climbie that looked into child protection issues and led to a review of such issues in the police and social services (Newburn et al. 2007).

Language Line: a commercial organization that provides 24-hour, 365-day-a-year language translation services either by telephone or face to face in over 100 languages. The language line is used by a range of organizations from the police service to the voluntary sector.

Lantern: a project led by PITO aimed to deliver a mobile fingerprint identity check in order to speed up the process of establishing a person's identity, thus allowing those operating the system to know whether an individual is wanted or dangerous.

LCJB: Local Criminal Justice Board; consisting of representatives from across the local justice sector, such as those from the police, prosecution services, courts system, victim support, probation, prisons and youth offending teams who together provide a local focus on how criminals are caught, convicted and rehabilitated along with the support available for victims and witnesses.

LCN DNA: low copy number DNA; a sensitive process for the recovery of DNA profiles from degraded or small amounts of DNA material, perhaps deposited at crime scenes (*see also* **DNA**).

Leading question: a question that suggests a specific answer, perhaps in a court of law or interview.

Learning diary: *see* **Reflective diary**.

Legal Aid: *see* **Criminal Defence Service**.

Legislation: a Bill that is heard and amended on a number of occasions before both Parliament and the House of Lords before being granted Royal Assent and becoming law.

Lesbian and Gay Police Association: formed in 1989 in order to provide support and advice to gay and lesbian officers (Loader and Mulcahy 2003).

Less than lethal weapon: a weapon such as a Taser, used by specially trained officers as an alternative to shooting with a firearm. A less than lethal weapon provides a means to incapacitate an individual demonstrating violent or aggressive behaviour rather than shooting and subsequently killing them (*see also* **Baton round** and **Taser**).

Levels of police response to intruder alarms: the Association of Chief Police Officers set out the levels of response that should be expected to activate intruder alarms; these are however adapted locally within police forces. These response levels of one, two and three are constantly reviewed. A level one response would, resources allowing, require an immediate response to the scene of the intruder alarm activation, a level two response would mean that a response would be routine in nature as and when resource allocation allows and a level three response is when the service provided of a response is withdrawn, this is usually due to a number of false activations (*see also* **URN**).

LGC Forensics: Laboratory of Government Chemists Forensics; one of the largest providers of forensic investigative techniques to law enforcement including DNA analysis, pathology, firearms and e-crime (*see also* **FSS**).

Licensing officer: working predominantly under the Licensing Act (2003), licensing officers can be police officers or civilian staff responsible for the investigation, authorization, education of clients and enforcement of licences for a range of applications from the sale of alcohol on premises to late-night refreshments.

Lie detector: *see* **Polygraph**.

Lima: a letter of the phonetic alphabet that is utilized to describe the letter L (*see* **Appendix 4**).

LIO: local intelligence officer; acting as a single point of reference for a local policing area, the LIO is responsible for analysing, identifying patterns and disseminating information and intelligence about criminals and criminal activity.

Livescan: the electronic computerized scanning of fingerprints of a detained person using a console held within a custody suite. Livescan links online to Ident 1 allowing the swift verification of a person's identity by comparison with over six million sets of fingerprints held and also allows an online comparison to be made with unidentified marks recovered from crime scenes (*see also* **Fingerprints, Ident 1** and **NAFIS**).

LMG: Leucomalachite Green; one of a number of commercially manu-factured presumptive blood testing kits that allows appropriately trained personnel, usually CSIs or forensic scientists, to swiftly distinguish between apparent blood and other red stains such as paint or brown boot polish (Pepper 2005) (*see also* **KM**).

Local Criminal Justice Board: represents the key local stakeholders in the criminal justice process ensuring a joint approach to dealing with crime and its outcomes.

Locard: a commercially produced computerized integrated evidence management system for use by a range of forensic practitioners.

Locard, Edmond: a late nineteenth- and early twentieth-century police employee, Edmond Locard was one of the first police forensic scientists and established the first forensic science laboratory in Lyon in order to examine fingerprints and other trace evidence recovered from crime scenes.

Loop: a pattern made up of the ridges found on a thumb or finger (*see also* **Fingerprints**).

Lost and found property: lost property is often reported to the police and should be accurately recorded in a register. Found property should also be recorded and is retained for a period of time before being disposed of, often through auctions.

LPG: legislation, procedures and guidance; how legislation, such as the Freedom of Information Act 2000, is embedded within force procedure with notes of guidance on its application and use.

LSD: lysergic acid diethylamide is an illegal drug usually impregnated into small white squares of card bearing popular designs such as cartoon characters. It is synthesized from lysergic acid, which comes from ergot, a fungus found on rye. Around 20 minutes after being taken orally (although it can be absorbed through the skin), the user experiences a range of effects depending on their mood, the environment and the dosage taken. Effects include hallucinations and heightened perceptions of colour and sound. The effects (trip) can last for up to five hours, but can have long-term emotional effects, with users reporting significant personality changes, and 'flashbacks' can happen years later.

M

MACC: Military aid to the civil community; practical support by the armed forces, such as personnel or helicopters, in order to assist the police during major incidents or disasters.

MacPherson Report: report published in 1999 into the murder of Stephen Lawrence in London during 1993 that concluded that there was institutional racism and professional incompetency within the police. The report recommended improvements in training in relation to cultural diversity, set targets for recruitment from ethnic minority groups and provided a definition for institutional racism (*see also* **Diversity, IAG** and **Scarman Report**).

Magistrate: a court official (*see* **JP**).

Magistrates Court: a criminal court in England and Wales, usually chaired by at least one magistrate, which is used to try less serious offences (*see also* **Court of Appeal, Crown Court, House of Lords** and **Queens Bench Division**).

Magna powder: a granular powder available in a range of colours used by CSIs to locate fingerprints.

Magneta flake powder: a silver-coloured flake powder used by CSIs to locate fingerprints.

MAIB: Marine Accident Investigation Branch; non-police organization within the Department for Transport with responsibility for the investigation of accidents and incidents involving ships from the UK on a worldwide basis and ships in UK waters. Their investigation does not aim to apportion blame but to prevent such accidents or incidents occurring again (MAIB 2006).

Major incident: a major incident is any emergency, such as a flood, explosion or oil spill, which requires the implementation of special plans and arrangements by one or a number of the emergency services, the National Health Service or local authority.

Major incident room: established as soon as possible after commencing an enquiry into a major incident, the major incident room is the focal point and administrative centre for the whole investigation. The major incident room is run along specific nationally agreed guidelines and is usually staffed with a specific specialist team including a senior investigating officer and his or her deputy, an office manager, readers (who read statements as they come in), indexers (who code information and raise actions to be completed), telephonists, and so on (*see also* **HOLMES II, Indexer** and **MIRSAP**).

MAPPA: Multi-Agency Public Protection Arrangement; MAPPA legislation came into force in April 2001 under sections 67 and 68 of the Criminal Justice and Court Services Act (2000). It grew out of working relationships between the police, probation and prison services, and brought these services together to act jointly as the 'Responsible Authority' to establish arrangements for assessing and managing the risks posed by certain sexual, violent and other dangerous offenders.

Marine Unit: A number of police forces have Marine Units (known as the River Police in the Metropolitan Police Service) that have specially equipped vessels staffed with specially trained police officers to patrol coastlines and inland waters, reassuring the public and enforcing the law. The Ministry of Defence police operate the largest marine unit patrolling military installations.

Marquis Reagent: a presumptive test for drugs that is approved for use by law enforcement agencies by the Home Office.

Mass murder: when a number of murders are committed in one event in a single area or location. An example of mass murder would be the shooting of 16 children and their teacher in Dunblane, Scotland by Thomas Hamilton in 1996 (*see also* **Corporate manslaughter, Homicide, Honour killing, Murder/Manslaughter, Murder manual, Serial killer** and **Spree killer**).

Mass screen: taking identifiable samples (e.g. DNA or fingerprints) from a large number of people in order to prove or disprove their involvement in an offence. Specific protocols must be adhered to ensuring accurate identification of the individual donor (e.g. photographic ID and interviews with neighbours) prior to taking the sample. The first DNA mass screen for the investigation of crime commenced in January 1987 to investigate and identify the perpetrator of two rapes and murders in the Midlands area of England. In several months the police had recovered and obtained the DNA profiles of over 4000 young males (Williams and Johnson 2008). The mass DNA screen failed to identify the perpetrator however when information came to light that an individual had falsely purported to be Colin Pitchfork when donating their DNA. This led to the arrest and eventual identification by DNA of the real Colin Pitchfork who was convicted for the rapes and murders in 1988. Forty years earlier, in 1948, the first fingerprint mass screen was conducted in order to identify the murderer of a young child who had been found in the grounds of Blackburn Hospital. The senior investigator requested that the fingerprints of all males between 14 and 90 and resident in Blackburn should be taken (Tullett 1981). Eventually, along with the use of other forensic evidence, the mass screen led to the arrest, conviction and hanging of the Blackburn resident Peter Griffiths for the murder (*see also* **DNA** and **Fingerprints**).

Matricide: the act of killing one's own mother (*see also* **Parricide** and **Patricide**).

MCA: Maritime and Coastguard Agency; the MCA is responsible to the government for saving lives on the coast and at sea, while ensuring the safety of vessels and the prevention of pollution of the sea and the coastline.

McNaghten Rules: rules suggesting that jurors in a trial set out to assume that the defendant is sane and has sufficient capacity to commit the crime until the contrary is proved, and also set out a number of points for the defendant to establish a defence of insanity.

MDAT: Major Disaster Advisory Team; a team of experienced police personnel who are available at short notice to provide advice and guidance on the management of incidents.

MDP: *see* **MOD Police**.

Media Advisory Group: an ACPO group providing advice and guidance to forces on dealing with the media (Newburn et al. 2007) (*see also* **CCU**).

Mens rea: literally meaning guilty mind, the mens rea is the psychological intention to commit a crime (*see* **Actus reus**).

Merlin: Missing Persons and Linked Indices police IT system initially designed for the Metropolitan Police Service.

Met: Metropolitan Police; the largest police force in the UK, first established in 1829, with responsibility for policing London. The force has over 50 000 employees made up of over 32 000 officers and 18 000 civilian staff (*see also* **Peel, Robert**).

Methadone: a synthetic drug, usually in the form of a syrup, which is a medically produced substitute for heroin.

Metropolitan Police Film Piracy Unit: a specialist police unit focused on combating the illegal production and distribution of pirated films (*see also* **FACT**).

MG forms: a range of forms from a manual of guidance used to create a case file relating to the investigation of an offence by the police and prosecution of the offender by the Crown Prosecution Service. The forms used to build the case file range from an MG1 being a front sheet, an MG11 witness statement form to an MG18 offences taken into consideration form (*see* **Appendix 2** for a complete list) (*see also* **Case file**).

Mike: a letter of the phonetic alphabet that is utilized to describe the letter M (*see* **Appendix 4**).

MIRSAP: Major Incident Room Standard Administrative Procedures; originally written by the Home Office and subsequently refined by ACPO. MIRSAP defines the nationally agreed standards and procedures used by investigators and administrators within a major incident room to divide responsibilities and make best use of information (*see also* **Major incident room** and **Murder manual**).

Miscarriage of justice: the miscarriages of justice that occur within the criminal justice system can be attributed to the fabrication of evidence or evidence not being disclosed, the validity of expert witnesses used within a trial, questionable techniques used to obtain confessions or the misidentifications of individuals. The contemporary concept of miscarriage of justice is based around events and developments in the 1980s and 1990s. Legislation has been introduced aiming to reduce miscarriages such as the Police and Criminal Evidence Act 1984, the Criminal Procedures and Investigation Act 1996 and established procedures, such as the standards used to identify fingerprints, have been reformed. A number of cases exemplify miscarriages of justice, such as the Birmingham six in 1974 and Shirley McKie in 1997. In 1974 pub bombings killed 21 people and injured over 160. Shortly afterwards six Irishmen were arrested on suspicion of the attacks, who in 1975 were found guilty and sentenced to life imprisonment. However, they were released in 1991 after appeal when forensic tests showed that police statements had been altered and the tests used for explosives could also have been positive due to the handling of cigarettes. In 1997 Shirley McKie was a member of a police team investigating the murder of Marion Ross in Scotland. A fingerprint recovered from the crime scene was identified by fingerprint experts as belonging to Shirley but in court she testified that it was not hers. She was arrested, charged with perjury and lost her job. In 1999 after hearing testimony from several other fingerprint experts, including two from the US, that the fingerprint was not hers, Shirley was acquitted (*see also* **Criminal Cases Review Commission** and **IPCC**).

Misdemeanour: a term used within the US justice system to describe a less serious crime (e.g. theft without violence), which attracts a punishment not exceeding one year of imprisonment (*see also* **Felony, Indictable offence** and **Summary offence**).

MISPER: a missing person.

MIT: Major Investigation Team/Murder Investigation Team; a team of detectives and specialist civilian staff who have sole responsibility, under the guidance of a senior investigating officer, for the investigation of serious crime, such as murder and manslaughter, within a particular force area and the conduct of cold case reviews (*see also* **Cold case review, Designated investigator, IO, SIO** and **TI**).

Mitochondrial DNA: DNA found outside the cell nucleus that is inherited from the mother.

MLP: multilocus probe; a forensic process for extracting DNA from good-quality crime scene samples.

MO: *modus operandi*; the way in which a crime is committed by a particular offender, such as the type of premises burgled, how entry was gained, the type of goods stolen, and so on.

Mobile data terminal: hand-held or vehicle-located computer terminals that allow law enforcement officers to search PNC and in force IT sources to personally check details of individuals and vehicles while on the street.

MOD: Ministry of Defence; the government department responsible for matters in relation to the defence of the UK as a whole and its interests overseas.

MOD Police: the Ministry of Defence Police is a large national police force that has the responsibility for policing and security of over 100 MOD establishments and personnel within their jurisdiction across the UK. It is also responsible for the provision of specialist policing on behalf of the government of the UK in a number of post-conflict regions across the world (e.g. Afghanistan and Kosovo). The MOD Police are supplemented in the UK with the MOD Guarding Agency that provides static security at a number of MOD sites (*see* **Appendix 1**).

MODACE: Management of Disasters and Civil Emergencies; a police training programme targeted at senior personnel who may be responsible for dealing with disasters and civil emergencies.

MoPI: Management of Police Information; with its roots in the Bichard report into the Soham murders, MoPI guidelines were designed to ensure that all relevant operational policing information held locally, regionally and nationally is recorded, shared, updated and deleted on a regular basis (*see also* **Bichard**).

Mounted Branch: a small specialist unit of police officers trained to work on horseback to conduct a range of duties from general patrol reassuring the public to the control of large crowds where the height of the police officer on horseback provides an excellent vantage point and feeling of police presence. The horses are also specially trained to deal with a range of unusual experiences, such as the loud noises created by gunshots or crowds, along with being able to deal with missiles that are thrown at them.

MRCC: Maritime Rescue Coordination Centre; a network of centres around the coast operated by the Maritime and Coastguard Agency providing 24-hour, 365-day-a-year monitoring, rescue initiation and coordination for those in difficulty and distress around the coasts of the UK.

MRT: mountain rescue team; MRTs provide mountain and fell search and rescue services, and respond to requests by the police to a range of incident types, such as a search for vulnerable missing people.

Murder/Manslaughter: the unlawful killing of a human being by a person of sound mind with or without the intent to kill them (*see also* **Corporate manslaughter, Homicide, Honour killing, Mass murder, Murder manual, Serial killer** and **Spree killer**).

Murder manual: the murder investigation manual, developed by the Association of Chief Police Officers and the National Centre for Policing Excellence, sets out guidance for investigators into how the investigation into a murder should be conducted (*see also* **Corporate manslaughter, Homicide, Honour killing, Mass murder, MIRSAP, Murder/Manslaughter, Serial killer** and **Spree killer**).

N

NaBID: National Ballistics Intelligence Database; an IT system that is used to identify intelligence in relation to incidents involving firearms and track evidence from scenes of shootings and the related firearms (*see also* **Ballistics** and **Firearm**).

NACRO: National Association for the Care and Resettlement of Offenders; a charity that works with ex-offenders, the disadvantaged and deprived to provide practical solutions, such as the facilitation of sporting activities, education and mediation, in order to reduce crime (NACRO 2004).

NaCTSO: National Counter Terrorism Security Office; a central police unit that has specialist staff who can provide guidance and advice on the security of chemical, biological and radiological material (NaCTSO 2007) (*see also* **CT, CTSA** and **CTU**).

NAFIS: National Automated Fingerprint Identification System; a commercially designed IT system facilitating the national computerization of fingerprint records. The system allows online verification of an individual's identity against a database of over six million sets of fingerprints, searching marks recovered from crime scenes against fingerprint records and checking fingerprint records against unidentified marks recovered from crime scenes. NAFIS has been superseded by Ident 1 (*see also* **Ident 1** and **Livescan**).

NARPO: National Association for Retired Police Officers; a national association that represents the interests of retired police officers and their widows, and provides support and advice.

NASCH: **N**ame, **A**ge, **S**ex, **C**olour and **H**eight; a mnemonic to assist in remembering the factors that are required for a person search on the Police National Computer (*see also* **PNC**).

National Core Competencies: a list of skills, knowledge, attitudes and behaviours drawn up by Skills for Justice into a behavioural framework that must be demonstrated in order to work as a police officer or community support officer. The list includes showing respect for race and diversity, team working, community and customer focus, personal responsibility and resilience, along with the ability to communicate effectively (*see also* **NCF** and **NOS**).

National Crime Recording Standard: a national standard for recording crimes in order to show consistency and provide transparency between the way police forces record crime. As such, any incident whether reported by a victim, witness or other person will initially be recorded and investigated as to whether it is a crime or not (*see also* **Home Office Counting Rules** and **Offence code**).

National Firearms Licensing Management System: first suggested as a result of the inquiry into the shooting of 16 children and their teacher in Dunblane during 1996, a national register of firearms was stipulated as a requirement under the Firearms (Amendment) Act 1997. The National Firearms Licensing Management System, first piloted across several police forces in 2006, now allows police forces to share information on legally held firearms.

National Institute of Justice: the National Institute of Justice conducts research within the US on behalf of the US Department of Justice.

National Offender Management Service: a department of the Ministry of Justice, the National Offender Management Service (NOMS) aims to manage convicted offenders both within the prison and the community supporting them in an effort to reduce reoffending.

National Policing Plan: the national targets and priorities for policing across England and Wales established by the Government and published by the Home Office on an annual basis.

National Status Codes: using the airwave radio network and a series of nationally recognized numbers relating to their status, officers can convey their duties and commitments (e.g. on duty, on route to scene, at court, etc.) to control rooms and colleagues.

NCALT: National Centre for Applied Learning Technologies; an online managed learning environment and specialist immersive learning designed in collaboration between the National Police Improvement Agency and the Metropolitan Police Service to provide learning packages for law enforcement personnel (NCALT 2008).

NCEC: National Chemical Emergency Centre; provides advice to enforcement agencies 24 hours a day on the safety of chemicals that may be involved in a hazardous situation, such as a leak or collision.

NCF: National Competency Framework; a management framework designed to identify the key and standard features of specific job roles (*see also* **National Core Competencies** and **NOS**).

NCOF: National Crime and Operations Faculty; a department within the National Police Improvement Agency, NCOF focuses on the provision of advice, guidance and specialist support for the investigation of crime and its reduction along with the policing of civil disorder.

NCPE: National Centre for Policing Excellence; part of the NPIA, the aim of the NCPE is to disseminate good practice to all forces.

NCRS: National Crime Recording Standards; a standard that applies exactly the same to all police forces in England and Wales and which sets out how and when forces record crime. Home Office records are updated annually according to the figures supplied by forces using these rules.

NECTU: National Extremism Tactical Coordination Unit; a Home Office-funded unit providing advice on the investigation and policing of domestic extremist activities (*see also* **DE**).

Needlestick injury: when a needle from a syringe injures an individual. Needlestick injuries do occur within the law enforcement community and this carries with it the risk of infection from a needle contaminated with a blood-borne disease. Although little empirical research exists relating to such injuries within the police service in the UK, research within the San Diego Police Department in the US suggests that a range of factors such as evening shifts, searches of individuals and inexperience all increase the risk of receiving such an injury (Lorentz et al. 2000).

Neighbourhood policing: seen by the government as one of the cornerstones of police reform and embedded in changes introduced within the Police Reform Act 2002. The aim of neighbourhood policing is to regain the trust and confidence of the general public using high-visibility local patrols, dealing with matters that concern the general public, such as public nuisance, and a return to a community policing model, long forgotten with the fading image of 'Dixon of Dock Green'. However, nowadays the neighbourhood policing model is based on a police officer managing a team of community support officers, special constables and wardens using their new skills, presence and powers, such as the ASBO, to reassure the public (McLaughlin 2007) (*see also* **Community-oriented policing, Crime warden, Dixon of Dock Green, Neighbourhood policing team, PCSO** and **Problem-oriented policing**).

Neighbourhood policing team: each BCU within a police force is sub-divided into areas of one or more council wards, each of which has its own neighbourhood policing team made up of police officers managing teams of community support officers, special constables and wardens (*see also* **Neighbourhood policing**).

Neighbourhood Watch: voluntary schemes first established in the 1980s in communities where volunteers work as coordinators and observers in partnership with the police to reduce crime (by increasing security) and the fear of crime by reassurance of safety within the community.

New Scotland Yard: originally a narrow lane in London to the rear of offices; established in 1829 for the first commissioners of the Metropolitan Police, and now synonymous with, and perhaps the most famous, police station within the Metropolitan Police Service.

NFA: no further action, the result of an enquiry.

NHS Counter Fraud and Security Management Service: a law enforcement organization within the National Health Service (NHS) responsible for the investigation and detection of fraud and corruption across the NHS and the development of associated measures of security.

NHTCU: National Hi-Tech Crime Unit; established in 2001 to police the internet in partnership with police forces across the UK (Jewkes 2007). NHTCU is now part of SOCA (*see also* **CEOPC** and **NSLEC**).

NIB: National Identification Bureau; a national criminal records bureau held by the Metropolitan Police Service (*see also* **CRO, NIS, Phoenix** and **PNC**).

Niche: commercially produced police records management system.

NIM: National Intelligence Model; a model devised within law enforcement that aims to make the best use of intelligence across all agencies. In the UK all forces were required by the Police Reform Act (2002) to adopt the National Intelligence Model by April 2004. It is based on the concept of intelligence-led policing that emphasizes the use of criminal intelligence when planning policing operations and tactics. The model is built on three levels of criminal activity: local confined to a single area or BCU (dealing with volume crime is a particular issue at this level); cross-border within multiple BCUs or cross-force (where key issues will be the identification of common problems, the exchange of data and information and the provision of resources); and serious and organized crime affecting national and international interests (at this level a proactive approach is required for identification of issues, leading to a response through targeted operations by dedicated units working at a national level). The intelligence model is built on a framework of best practice and cooperation between police forces and other agencies. There is a heavy emphasis on the tasking and coordination process, whereby intelligence work is prioritized and intelligence produced is studied by a tasking and coordination group chaired by a senior officer, who direct the policing effort and allocate resources. When utilized correctly, the National Intelligence Model links business planning directly with operational policing. It links intelligence, crime prevention and enforcement at local, regional and national levels (NCIS 2000) (*see also* **ANACAPA, Crime pattern analysis, Five** × **five intelligence, Intelligence, Intelligence analyst, Intelligence cycle, Intelligence-led policing** and **Watson**).

Ninhydrin: chemical used to develop fingerprints on surfaces such as paper.

NIP: Notice of Intended Prosecution; details presented either verbally or in writing of an intention to prosecute an individual who is suspected of an offence, such as dangerous or careless driving.

NIS: National Identification Service; a national records office that deals with all enquiries for identification ranging from emigration requests to Freedom of Information Acts requests for information held on the Police National Computer (*see also* **NIB**).

NMIS: National Management Information System; a commercially produced IT system that can interrogate information held across the 43 Home Office police forces across England and Wales to identify a range of statistical information from crime trends to officer numbers.

NMPH: National Missing Persons Helpline; established in 1992 NMPH maintains a detailed missing persons' database and aims to advise and support both missing people and those who are missing them.

Non-endorsable offences: offences, such as illegal parking, which may result in a fine for the motorist but no endorsement of an individual's driving licence with penalty points (*see also* **Endorsable offences**).

Non-Home Office force: a police force, such as the Ministry of Defence Police, which has no direct accountability to the Home Office; instead, reporting to another government department or authority (*see* **Appendix 1** for a full list of non-Home Office forces).

Non-intimate samples: under the Police and Criminal Evidence Act (1984) and the Criminal Justice and Police Act (2001) non-intimate samples can be taken by a police officer or appropriately designated individual (e.g. a detention officer) from a person with consent, or with an inspector's authority without consent. Samples can include hair with root and hair combings (not pubic), saliva, earprints and footprints (*see also* **Buccal cells, DNA, Intimate samples, Intimate search** and **Plucked head hair**).

NOS: National Occupational Standards; these have been designed and written by Skills for Justice in consultation with subject experts and practitioners. They are regularly reviewed in order to ensure they meet the needs of policing. NOS define the standards that must be achieved to perform a particular role. Probationary police officers must achieve 22 NOS (*see* **Appendix 3** for a complete list) in order to demonstrate their occupational competency to carry out their duties effectively. Police community support officers and special constables must achieve a reduced number of these competencies. Alternative law enforcement careers (e.g. fingerprint officers and crime scene investigators) have their own role-specific national occupational standards to achieve. The NOS to be achieved by police officers include the ability for them to demonstrate that they use actions in a fair and justified way, provide initial responses to incidents and then present detained persons to custody (*see also* **National Core Competencies, NCF, Skills for Justice** and **Skillsmark**).

Notice of Intended Prosecution: either a written or verbal warning that it is the intention of the police/CPS to prosecute the recipient of the letter or warning for the offence detailed.

November: a letter of the phonetic alphabet that is utilized to describe the letter N (*see* **Appendix 4**).

NPIA: National Police Improvement Agency; established in April 2007 with the amalgamation of a number of existing police agencies, such as Centrex and PITO, NPIA aims to deliver effective, efficient and up-to-date training and educational programmes to the police across England and Wales while developing leading-edge information and communication technology solutions for modern policing.

NPP: National Policing Plan; a plan produced by the Home Office every three years detailing the targets, expectations and developments that are expected of the police service across England and Wales.

NPT: *see* **Neighbourhood policing team**.

NSCAS: National Senior Careers Advisory Service; an initiative aimed at ensuring that the pool of officers with the appropriate skills and knowledge at a senior level within the police organization, particularly those from under-represented minority groups, better represents the communities they serve.

NSLEC: National Specialist Law Enforcement Centre; part of the National Hi-Tech Crime Unit, NSLEC is responsible for designing and delivering up-to-date knowledge and skills to law enforcement personnel in relation to hi-tech and computer crime (*see* **CEOPC** and **NHTCU**).

NSPCC: National Society for the Prevention of Cruelty to Children; founded in the nineteenth century, the NSPCC looks after the interests of children, the young and their families, such as operating a child protection helpline and lobbying parliament for changes in legislation (NSPCC 2006).

NSPIS: National Strategy for Police Information Systems; an integrated IT system that deals with processing and sharing case material throughout the criminal justice process from arrest to prosecution. The Narey report 1997 reviewed and provided recommendations on the speed with which cases were taken through the criminal justice system. One recommendation highlighted was the need for the integrated IT system that now consists of numerous linked IT systems including those responsible for personnel records, case preparation, command and control and custody.

NTCSSI: National Training Centre for Scientific Support to Crime Investigation; a training centre in the north of England, which is part of the NPIA and specializes in the education and training of crime scene investigators from across the UK.

NTO: National Training Organization; a number of NTOs were established by the Department for Education and Employment to represent and develop employers and those employed within the workplace, such as the Further Education National Training Organization (FENTO) (*see also* **Sector Skills Council** and **Skills for Justice**).

NTSB: National Transportation Safety Board; the US Agency responsible for the investigation of accidents and subsequent safety recommendations within the US transportation infrastructure at home and abroad (*see also* **AAIB, MAIB** and **RAIB**).

NVC: non-verbal communication; a skill developed with experience to recognize the non-verbal communications (body language), which may influence how you deal with or interpret an individual, such as the lack of eye contact or folded arms appearing suspicious. However, different cultures can require alternative interpretations of the NVCs.

NVQ: National Vocational Qualification; a nationally recognized qualification that can be used to demonstrate competency to perform specific tasks within the workplace. NVQs can be achieved by officers during their probationer training as part of the Initial Police Learning and Development Programme (IPLDP) or when taking up specialist roles such as management (*see also* **Foundation degree** and **IPLDP**).

Nylon bag: a bag used to package samples from fire scenes or clothing from suspects for arson cases to ensure the volatile vapours from accelerants (e.g. petrol) are retained for later forensic examination at a laboratory (*see also* **Accelerants**).

NYP: North Yorkshire Police (*see* **Appendix 1**).

O

Oath: a statement made orally by a witness in a court of law in the form of an oath or affirmation stating that the evidence they give are the facts as they perceive them.

OCU: Operational Command Unit; generic term used to describe a unit within the Metropolitan Police tasked with specific roles and responsibilities, such as the Transport OCU having responsibility for the policing of the road and bus network across London (*see also* **BCU**).

Occupational Health: a department within each police force that provides occupational health services (ranging from dealing with injuries while on duty to assessments of fitness to work) by qualified and experienced health care professionals.

Offence: when a crime has been committed.

Offence code: unique national codes that relate to specific offence types, such as SP30 (speeding on a public road), which aid in the distinction between offences and provision of an accurate measure of the types of offence being committed (*see also* **BVPI** and **NCRS**).

Offences brought to justice: performance indicators measuring the number of convictions, cautions, reprimands, warnings and fixed penalty notices dealt with by the criminal justice system (*see also* **Home Office Counting Rules** and **KPI**).

Offensive weapon: originally defined in the Prevention of Crime Act (1953) and amended on several occasions. An offensive weapon is any item made (e.g. a knife), adapted (e.g. a sharpened heel of a stiletto) or intended (e.g. a screwdriver carried without legitimate reason) carried in a public place with the intention of causing an injury or harm.

Office for Criminal Justice Reform: established to ensure that the general public have confidence in a joined-up and effective criminal justice system, the Office of Criminal Justice Reform consists of a multidisciplinary team from the Ministry of Justice, Home Office and the Office of the Attorney General (Flanagan 2008).

OIC: officer in the case; the law enforcement officer who takes responsibility for leading enquiries and collating information in relation to the case, such as building the case file, until it is concluded (*see also* **IO**).

OP: observation post; a location from where it is possible to observe the local area.

Open court: a court hearing held in public (*see* **In camera**).

Opinion evidence: when a witness provides an opinion in a criminal court based on their personal experience and expertise in the subject (Hannibal and Mountford 2002).

OPL: over the prescribed limit; when a person attempts to drive a motor vehicle on a road, or in a public place, with the amount of alcohol in his or her system exceeding the prescribed limit (Road Traffic Act 1988). The limits of alcohol for offences under the Road Traffic Act 1988 are: in breath (35 micrograms of alcohol per 100 millilitres of breath), a blood sample (80 milligrams of alcohol per 100 millilitres of blood) or sample of urine (107 micrograms of alcohol in 100 millilitres of urine). The Railways and Transport Safety Act 2003 also defines offences for being over the prescribed limit when in control of other forms of transport; for example, the blood/alcohol limit for aircrew is 20 milligrams of alcohol per 100 millilitres of blood. A sample of blood for analysis can only be taken by an appropriate health care professional such as a forensic medical examiner (*see also* **FME, Hip flask defence** and **Intoximeter**).

Opsline: operated by the National Centre for Policing Excellence (*see* **NCPE**), Opsline operators provide advice and guidance to investigators and uniformed officers on operational policing issues. The Opsline initiative is also responsible for ensuring that a database of expert advisers is maintained for the police service.

Organized crime: broadly, organized crime is any illegal enterprise operating across territorial boundaries, which could be regional or national, by a number of individuals operating within a structured and hierarchical organization whose main goal is the generation of profit (*see also* **SCDEA, SOCA** and **Transnational policing**).

Original notes: in order for notes to be original they should be those notes made by the law enforcement officer at the time, or as soon as practicably possible after he or she has attended the occurrence, incident or crime. Original notes can take many forms ranging from the law enforcement officer's pocket notebook, property log, CSI report form, computer log, and so on (*see also* **Contemporaneous notes**).

OS: Ordnance Survey; the organization responsible for the production of up-to-date detailed digital and physical maps.

Oscar: a letter of the phonetic alphabet that is utilized to describe the letter O (*see* **Appendix 4**).

OSCE: Organization for Security and Co-operation in Europe; relying in a large part on secondments of experienced law enforcement practitioners from police forces across the UK and Europe, OSCE is an organization that has championed human rights and ethical policing through the establishment of police training centres across regions of the world, which are ethically diverse and politically unstable or political instability is nearby (Wright 2006).

OSPRE: Objective Structured Performance Related Examination; the trademark name of the official examinations used by the police for promotion to sergeant and then inspector. The examinations consist of two parts: a knowledge section from a set syllabus and a competency section that matches the required skills to the Integrated Competency Framework (*see also* **ICF**).

OST: officer safety training; superseded in general terms by the term personal safety training (*see also* **PST**).

Out of court disposal: seen as an alternative to prosecution, various means of out of court disposal are available to officers, and to a lesser extent community support officers, to deal with low-risk and low-level crime usually committed by first-time offenders. The decision to deal with the offence outside of a court can lead to the officer taking no further action, giving an informal warning, a cannabis warning or penalty notice for disorder. The disposal must be seen by the officer as justified, appropriate and a proportionate way of dealing with the offence.

P

PAA: Police Athletics Association; an association aimed at encouraging sporting activities throughout the police service whether at competition level or for self-development.

PACE: Police and Criminal Evidence Act 1984; one of the primary pieces of legislation that sought to formalize and regulate police practices. The application of PACE (and the subsequent legislation that has amended its application, such as the Serious Organized Crime and Police Act (2005), is supported by regularly updated codes of practice that interpret and detail the practical applications of the legislation (*see also* **Code of Practice**).

PACRAM: procedures and communications to be used in the case of a release of radioactive material. In the case of an unexpected atmospheric pollution caused by the release of radioactive material whether within the UK or threatening the UK from abroad, the meteorological office will provide the emergency services with a weather forecast, predictions on dispersions of material, and so on (Met Office 2007) (*see also* **CHEMET**).

PACS: Police Action Checklists; this is a formalized collection of evidence (often in the form of a portfolio cross referenced to the National Occupational

Standards) to demonstrate that a student police officer is ready and able to perform independent patrol (*see also* **Independent patrol, NOS, Reflective diary** and **SOLAP**).

Papa: a letter of the phonetic alphabet that is utilized to describe the letter P (*see* **Appendix 4**).

Parricide: the act of killing a close relative (*see also* **Matricide** and **Patricide**).

Pathologist: a forensic pathologist is a highly skilled and trained clinical pathologist who has specialized in the investigation of sudden and unexplained deaths. A forensic pathologist will usually, on request of the police investigative team, attend the scene of a sudden or unexplained death, and after the body has been recovered to a mortuary, conduct the post-mortem (autopsy). The pathologist can often indicate an approximation of a time of death and the probable cause.

Patricide: the act of killing one's father (*see also* **Matricide** and **Parricide**).

PC: police constable; a police constable is appointed to protect life and property, maintain order, along with the prevention and detection of crime. On appointment constables swear allegiance to the Crown (*see also* **Constable**).

PCA: Police Complaints Association (*see* **Independent Police Complaints Commission – IPCC**).

PCR: polymerase chain reaction; a chemical reaction that produces a copy of the DNA strand. The process is used to multiply the amount of DNA available for analysis, enabling DNA profiles to be obtained from much smaller samples.

PCSO: police community support officer; a role established by the Police Reform Act (2002). PCSOs are uniformed officers employed by the police authority who provide a high-visibility presence within the community to reassure the general public and deter the commission of crime. PCSOs often deal with minor incidents such as public nuisance and criminal damage (*see also* **Crime warden** and **Neighbourhood policing**).

PD: physical developer; a chemical process used by specialist forensic investigators to develop fingerprints on porous surfaces such as paper.

PDP: personal development plan; a record of action planning written and maintained by a probationary police officer in consultation with their lecturers and tutor constables, which through reflection identifies the goals that the student officer intends to achieve and the actions he or she must conduct in order to achieve those goals (Bullock and Jamieson 1998).

PDR: performance and development review; a system of checking on a regular basis (often annually by a line manager) that an individual is professionally up to date and to identify the development and training opportunities required in order to continue in his or her current role, and if desired develop the knowledge and skills for an alternate role within the organization.

PDU: Professional Development Unit; a training and assessment unit within the operational environment that supports student probationary police officers in their first months of operational and independent patrol (*see also* **Tutor constable**).

PEACE: a mnemonic relating to a model designed to assist officers when conducting an interview, which was first introduced to the police across England and Wales in 1992 (Dando et al. 2008). The interviewer should work through the following: **P** – Plan and prepare for the interview, considering questions to be asked and evidence to be presented, and so on; **E** – Engage and explain to the person being interviewed the process and purpose of the interview; **A** – Account, clarify and challenge the account given by the interviewee; **C** – Closure when the interviewer finishes the interview; **E** – Evaluate the account given by the interviewee, how it relates to the inquiry and reflect on what could be done differently on another occasion (*see also* **Cognitive interview** and **Reid technique**).

Peel, Robert: former Home Secretary and founder in 1829 of the Metropolitan Police. Peel's vision of an effective police service for the London area led to him establishing the precedent that the service reported directly to the Home Secretary and as such police constables were called 'bobbies' and 'peelers' by some members of the general public (*see also* **Constable, Colquhoun, Patrick** and **Fielding, John and Henry**).

Perjury: defined within the Perjury Act 1911, perjury occurs if an individual witness (or an interpreter) makes a statement during judicial proceedings that they know or suspect is not true (*see also* **Contempt of court**).

Persistent offender: a person aged 18 or over who has been charged and convicted of at least six offences in the previous 12 months.

PESTEL: Political, Economic, Social, Technological, Environmental and Legal; a management tool used to analyse and highlight potential future challenges (*see also* **Environmental scanning**).

Phoenix: Police and Home Office Enhanced Nominal Index; an IT system forming an element of the Police National Computer. Phoenix first became operational in 1995 (Thomas 2007) and holds the names, addresses, detailed descriptions and intelligence on individuals that have been dealt with for any offence by the police; this information can be easily searched (Povey 2000) (*see also* **Control room, CRO, Distinguishing marks, Phoenix source document, PNC** and **Vehicle online descriptive search**).

Phoenix source document: this document is completed each and every time an individual is arrested for the commission of an offence. The form includes the details and description of the offence along with a personal description of the person in custody, including tattoos. It is this information that can be searched via Phoenix (*see also* **Arrest summons number (ASN), Phoenix** and **PNC**).

Phonetic alphabet: standard words used to describe letters such as in radio transmissions (*see* **Appendix 4**).

PI: Performance Indicator (*see* **KPI**).

PIP: Professional Investigation Process; a national scheme aimed at enhancing investigative procedures for all officers and police staff involved in the process of investigation. There are four levels with level one completed by all police officers and civilian staff dealing with volume crime to level four training and assessment targeted at strategic officers investigating complex and/or protracted crimes.

PIRT: police initial recruitment test; assessments sat during the recruitment stage by potential and aspiring police officers. These five individually assessed tests involve checking the accuracy of information, numerical problems, spelling and sentence construction, logical reasoning and observing and recalling detail (*see also* **Job-related fitness test** and **SEARCH assessment**).

PITO: Police Information Technology Organization; provides IT products (e.g. NAFIS) and communications products (e.g. Airwave) to law enforcement agencies across the UK.

PLAN: a mnemonic for officers to use when deciding whether or not to use force in a situation such as making an arrest. The mnemonic stands for **P**roportionate, **L**egality, **A**ccount and **N**ecessary (*see also* **Use of force**).

Plea: a plea is made by one person to another, usually guilty or not guilty.

PLG: private and light goods; a classification for vehicles.

Plucked head hair: can be taken as a non-intimate sample under the Police and Criminal Evidence Act (1984) for DNA profiling. Roots need to be present on the plucked head hair for a successful DNA profile (*see also* **Buccal cells, Buccal swabs, DNA** and **Non-intimate sample**).

Plural policing: a term used to encompass the wider police family (e.g. community support officers) and the large range of other enforcement organizations (e.g. private security companies) used to police public and private spaces in order to ensure compliance with the law and provide both order and safety (Crawford et al. 2005). The large shopping mall at the Metro Centre in Gateshead is a good example of plural policing and has been used as a case study to conduct research into its effectiveness. The mall has hundreds of retail outlets, spread over several miles of shop frontage, attracts over 25 million visitors annually and deals with tens of thousands of vehicles daily. The shopping centre finances a team of Northumbria police officers to patrol this privately owned space who work in close partnership with a much larger number of private security staff, both those employed by the Metro Centre and those employed by individual retail outlets, who together provide high-visibility patrols, crime prevention and the investigation of crime within the confines of the mall, its outlets and car parks (ibid.) (*see also* **Community-oriented policing** and **Project Griffin**).

PM: post-mortem examination; an examination conducted by a pathologist of the body of a deceased, commencing with an external examination followed by the internal examination of the body and the removal of samples for further investigation (*see also* **Hyoid bone, Hypostasis** and **Rigor mortis**).

PMAS: Police Mutual Assurance Society; a 'friendly society' that provides financial investments and services solely to the wider police family.

PNB: Police Negotiating Board; a section of the Police Federation, the Police Negotiating Board was established in the 1980s to represent officers on the issues of pay, pensions and allowances (*see also* **Police Staff Council**).

PNC: Police National Computer; PNC first became available for use by the police service in 1974 with the details of registered vehicles. This was then extended to include indexes of fingerprints and names (Thomas 2007). PNC has been continually evolved and today with its Phoenix interface contains details of names, vehicles, property, DNA samples, and so on and all transactions that have taken place using the system from any of its 30 000 terminals (ibid.), such as when a person is stopped and searched or has their DNA taken (*see also* **Arrest summons number (ASN), CRO, Phoenix, Phoenix source document** and **Vehicle online descriptive search**).

PND: penalty notice for disorder; established under the Criminal Justice and Police Act (2001) police officers, and to a lesser extent community support officers, can issue penalty notices if he or she believes an offence within the schedule has been committed. These allow the payment of a fine without the individual attending court.

PNLD: Police National Legal Database; established in 1994, PNLD continues to supply up-to-date computerized legal information, case law and other legal information to all 43 police forces across England and Wales and other criminal justice organizations (Police National Legal Database 2005).

PNN2 and PNN3: Police National Network; a secure IT network linking police forces and the wider criminal justice system.

Pocket notebook: the main purpose of the pocket notebook is to provide a written document used by the law enforcement officer to record accurately all activities and actions taken while on duty. The pocket notebook can be used as evidence in a court of law and may also be used to demonstrate a law enforcement officer's integrity, reliability and professionalism (*see also* **ELBOWS**).

POE: point of entry or egress; the way that an offender has entered or exited a premises.

POLAC: slang for police accident; an accident involving a police vehicle or a vehicle driven by a police officer or civilian member of staff while on duty.

Police authority: each police force must have a police authority drawn from members of the community that is being policed. The authority is responsible for the continued running of an efficient and effective service and forms one of the tripartite arrangements for governing the force; the others being the Chief Constable and the Home Office .

Police Federation: the Police Federation can trace its origins back to the Police Act 1919. It represents the needs of all police officers across England and Wales up to and including the rank of chief inspector. The Federation cannot affiliate itself to any political organization or call for officers to take industrial action. The federation has representatives on a national board from all policing regions and negotiates on behalf of officers on conditions such as pay and pensions (*see also* **Edmund Davies report, JBB** and **Unison**).

Police Ombudsman for Northern Ireland: an independent body responsible for investigating complaints made against members of the Police Service of Northern Ireland by the general public (*see also* **PSNI**).

Police search team: a team of specially trained police officer search specialists who are utilized at incidents to thoroughly search houses, and so on for physical evidence (*see also* **POLSA**).

Police Staff College: established in 1949 (Loader and Mulcahy 2003) and now part of NPIA, the Police Staff College at Bramshill in Hampshire educates and trains the senior and future leaders of the police service. This is predominantly achieved through the senior command course.

Police Staff Council: negotiates on behalf of civilian police staff across England and Wales, outside of the Metropolitan Police area, on conditions of service and pay that are then recommended to chief constables but cannot be enforced (Flanagan 2008) (*see also* **PNB**).

Police Standards Unit: established within the Home Office in 2001 the Police Standards Unit monitors performance in an effort to raise standards and police performance.

Policing Performance and Assessment Framework: an ambitious Home Office project to develop measures to better reflect the role of the contemporary police service. In this way it will be possible to compare the service provided to the general public by police forces around the four key areas of crime reduction, crime investigation, public safety and the provision of assistance.

POLSA: police search adviser; a specially trained police officer responsible for providing advice and guidance on searching (*see also* **Police search team**).

Polygraph: a controversial forensic technique first introduced in the 1920s that uses equipment to measure changes in blood pressure, pulse rate, respiration and the skin to identify if the subject is telling lies (Lane 1992).

POP: *see* **Problem-oriented policing**.

Poroscopy: the examination of pores on the ridges of fingerprints to aid in the process of identification (*see also* **Fingerprints**).

Ports officer: a police officer based with a policing team at one of the UK's ports (e.g. Port of Bristol) to work with the wider port authorities to police the people and freight moving through the port area (*see also* **Border Agency** and **Special Branch**).

Ports unit: *see* **Ports officer**.

Posen inquiry: a report commissioned by the Home Office and completed in 1995 that examined the core and ancillary tasks completed by police officers and making recommendations of those tasks that could be conducted instead by local authorities or private agencies.

PoVA: *see* **Protection of Vulnerable Adults Scheme**.

PPE: personal protective equipment; clothing and equipment supplied to ensure the safety and well-being of an individual, such as fluorescent jackets or respirators (*see also* **Body armour**).

PPP: Public Private Partnership; strategic business partnerships to assist in the finance, building and running of resources such as police stations.

PRA: Police Reform Act 2002; the Act had a wide-ranging impact on policing ranging from the need for the government to produce and regularly update a National Policing Plan, which was to provide the direction for policing, to the introduction of powers for police community support officers.

Precept (police): the annual amount paid by householders towards policing as part of their council tax contributions.

PreCons: previous convictions that have been recorded.

Press Office: *see* **CCU**.

PRG: Police Research Group (superseded by RDS).

PRINCE: Projects in Controlled Environments; an IT system used for project management.

Printscan: a commercial product that can be used to overtly copy the footwear of prisoners or those whose footwear needs to be eliminated from an investigation (*see also* **Footwear evidence**).

PRISM: a commercially produced computerized integrated evidence management system used to track photographic evidence within a photographic department.

Prisoner: a person whose liberty has been taken away and who has been placed into custody.

Prisoner processing unit: usually staffed by a joint police and civilian custody assistants team, the prisoner processing unit deals with those in custody from their arrival at the custody suite, such as recording an individual's details, followed by taking photographs, fingerprints and DNA samples, thus releasing the arresting police officers to return to patrol (*see also* **Custody assistant, Custody officer** and **Custody suite**).

Probationer police officer: a newly appointed police officer must serve satisfactorily in their post as a probationary police officer for two years completing all training/education and being assessed as competent in all 22 National Occupational Standards at the end of which they are confirmed in their post as police officers (*see also* **Community placement, Independent patrol, IPLDP, NOS, Reflective diary, Regulation 13** and **SOLAP**).

Problem-oriented policing (POP): problem-oriented policing is based on the concepts of a US academic. Newburn (2003) highlights that POP focuses on identifying specific problems within the community and working methodically towards solving these issues with a realization that enforcement on its own will not resolve the problem (*see also* **Community-oriented poli-cing, Intelligence-led policing, Neighbourhood policing** and **SARA**).

Procurator fiscal: a member of the judiciary working within the Scottish legal system.

Professional standards: a department within each police force staffed by experienced investigators. Professional standards departments deal with complaints against law enforcement personnel and issues of discipline and misconduct.

Project Griffin: originally established in London during 2004 to bring together agencies such as the police, fire, ambulance, local authorities and private security providers (e.g. airport and shopping centre security staff) who need to work together in order to deter and conduct proactive operations in an attempt to identify and defeat terrorist and extremist activities. Project Griffin, an excellent example of plural policing within the contemporary environment, has now been extended to a number of other police forces across the country and continues to raise awareness of terrorism, collect, collate and share intelligence, foster trust and collaborative working across the emergency services, safety and security industries (*see also* **Plural policing**).

Property clerk: a civilian employee of the police force responsible for the accurate logging and secure storage of all items of property handed to them.

Protection of Vulnerable Adults Scheme: a national register of vul-nerable adults who have been abused or harmed (*see also* **ViSOR**).

PSDB: Police Scientific Development Branch; a policing organization employing scientists, researchers and police officers developing equipment solutions to policing challenges, such as the best paint scheme for police helicopters to the best brush to use with fingerprint powders.

PSNI: Police Service of Northern Ireland; established in 2001 the service has responsibility for policing the geographical area of Northern Ireland (*see* **Appendix 1**) (*see also* **FSA** and **Police Ombudsman for Northern Ireland**).

PSRCS: Public Safety Radio Communications System; a secure network for the emergency services that uses similar technology to mobile telephones to transmit and receive voice and data communication (*see also* **Airwave**).

PSSO: Police Skills and Standards Organization (superseded by Skills for Justice).

PST: Personal Safety Training; specialist practical skills taught, and regularly refreshed, to police officers and other specialist staff who deal with confrontational situations (e.g. PCSOs), providing them with the ability to protect themselves and others along with how to use reasonable force to make an arrest. The specialist PST team also usually administer the job-related fitness tests to potential and new recruits (*see also* **Job-related fitness test** and **OST**).

PSU: Police Support Unit or Police Standards Unit; Police Support Units are teams of specially trained officers strategically deployed with riot shields, helmets, flameproof suits, and so on to deal with public disorder. The Police Standards Unit was established in the Home Office in 2001 to identify issues within policing that could only be resolved by new or amended legislation (McLaughlin 2007).

PSV: public service vehicle; a classification for vehicles.

PTC: Police Training Centre; a number of police forces maintain their own training centres; some to deliver initial police training and others to deliver continuous professional development for both police and civilian staff.

PTDB: Police Training and Development Board; established in 2002 in order to review and evolve nationally police training and development.

PTI: physical training instructor; usually a police employee responsible within a police force for taught physical training sessions including job-related fitness testing such as the bleep running and grip tests.

PTP: probationer training programme; a two-year structured programme of study and operational practice, often culminating in the award of a Foundation degree or NVQs, which is then acknowledged by the individual police force by confirming the probationer in the post of a police officer (*see also* **Foundation degree, IPLDP, NVQ** and **Probationer police officer**).

PTSD: post-traumatic stress disorder; after a traumatic event it is possible to experience subsequent psychological and/or biological responses to that incident. Such responses can include changes in emotions, reoccurrence of images and avoiding certain situations. After the civil disturbances in Los Angeles during April 1992 research conducted of a number of the police officers directly involved found that of 141 respondents 17 per cent experienced varying degrees of PTSD (Harvey-Lintz and Tidwell 1997) (*see also* **Critical incident debriefing**).

Public order training: training officers and surveillance specialists as coordinated teams able to control and quell public disorder (*see also* **Riot** and **Riot shield**).

Pursuit: usually referred to in the terms of 'pursue and pursuit', this is when a specially trained police officer indicates for a driver to stop and he or she has the opportunity to do so, but then he or she continues driving in such a manner that the police driver believes there is no intention of the vehicle stopping as requested and the police driver continues behind the vehicle in order to either report its progress or to stop it (ACPO 2007b). A police driver must consider the implications of such a pursuit in relation to the apprehension of the offender versus the health and safety of people in the vicinity, including the driver failing to stop (*see also* **Boxing, Roads Policing Unit** and **Rolling block**).

PYO: persistent young offender; a young person under the age of 17 who has been charged and sentenced in a criminal court on several occasions (*see also* **Recidivist** and **Youth offending team**).

Q

QA: quality assurance; ensuring that a service or product provided is fit for purpose and meets the expectations of the customer.

QGM: Queens Gallantry Medal; a silver, circular medal with a blue and grey ribbon with a narrow pink stripe, introduced as a medal below that of the George Cross for acts of bravery by civilians or military personnel in certain circumstances. This may be worn on the police uniform (*see also* **George Cross** and **QPM**).

QPM: Queens Police Medal; a silver, circular medal with a blue and white ribbon with narrow red stripes, introduced in the 1950s for police officers who have demonstrated distinguished service or gallantry. The medal may be worn on the police uniform (*see also* **George Cross** and **QGM**).

Quasar: a very intense source of light that can be used by specially trained personnel to search for fingerprints, and other evidence such as fibres, using different wavelengths of light.

Quash: the overruling of a previous court decision by another court.

Quebec: a letter of the phonetic alphabet that is utilized to describe the letter Q (*see* **Appendix 4**).

Queens Bench Division: one of the three high courts (the others being the Family Division and the Chancery Division) that hears appeals from the lower courts (e.g. Crown Courts) on legal issues (*see also* **Court of Appeal, Crown Court, House of Lords** and **Magistrates Court**).

Queens Counsel: often referred to as QC, Queens Counsel is awarded to barristers who have demonstrated an excellent level of professional expertise in court.

Quick cuffs: *see* **Handcuffs**.

R

Racist incident: a racist incident is any occurrence, in the form of conduct, spoken or written words or actual practices, which any person, such as the victim or a witness, believes to be racist (ACPO 2000) (*see also* **RMI form**).

RAFP: Royal Air Force Police; provides security, policing and investigative services to all Royal Air Force personnel and establishments around the world (*see* **Appendix 1**).

RAIB: Rail Accident Investigation Branch; non-police organization reporting to the Department for Transport. RAIB have specialist skills in the investigation of accidents and incidents on the railways across the UK and also rail systems in the channel tunnel, underground and certain gauges of recreational and restored railways. Their aim is to improve safety and prevent similar accidents occurring in the future but not to apportion blame (RAIB 2007).

RAYNET: Radio Amateurs Emergency Network; an association that allows amateur radio enthusiasts to assist the emergency services during times of emergency by passing on messages.

RCMP: Royal Canadian Mounted Police; able to trace its roots back to the 1870s, the RCMP provides national policing across Canada with a focus on organized crime, crimes within the economy, terrorist activity, and fostering improved relations with aboriginal communities and the youth of Canada (RCMP 2007).

RD: rest day; a day off work.

RDS: Research, Development and Statistics Directorate of the Home Office; RDS employs statisticians, researchers, and so on in order to provide a statistics and publications service to ministers and decision makers within the Home Office and those within the criminal justice system on issues relating to crime, drug use, the prisons, and so on (Research, Development and Statistics 2007).

Reasonable grounds for suspicion: an officer must believe that there is something suspicious that would stand an objective evaluation by another reasonable person. This suspicion may be based on what the office has **S**een, **H**eard (a window breaking), what **A**ctions the individual took on the approach of the officer, something they said in **C**onversation with the officer, what the officer **K**new of the person in or location in relation to intelligence or an noxious **S**mell (e.g. petrol on a suspected arsonist). An often referred to mnemonic to assist in remembering the key words of seen, heard, actions, conversation, knew and smell is SHACKS.

Recidivist: a repeat or habitual offender. There are a number of factors that indicate the likelihood of an individual committing a repeat offence including the age of the offender, the type of offence committed and a previous history of convictions. For example, the reconviction rates of juveniles aged between 10 and 16 in Northern Ireland released from a justice centre during 2001 was 36 per cent within a year and nearly doubled in two years (Decodts 2005) (*see also* **PYO**).

Record of taped interview: a summary of the relevant points from the interview with a defendant.

Red diesel: fuel used for agricultural and industrial purposes that is exempt for the purposes of tax.

Reflective diary: part of the IPLDP training process and forming part of the SOLAP, the reflective diary is used by trainee police officers to record personal reflections on learning, how the learning could be applied in the workplace and to identify individual ongoing learning and development requirements throughout their time as a probationary police officer (*see also* **IPLDP, PACS, Probationer police officer** and **SOLAP**).

Reflex: a multi-agency task force on organized immigration crime.

Registered sex offender: an individual who has been convicted of a sexual offence (e.g. rape) and his or her name is included on the national register of sex offenders, which was established as a result of the Sex Offenders Act 1997 (*see also* **Sexual offences** and **Sexual Offences Prevention Order**).

Regulation 9 notice: a notice to a police officer of an investigation being conducted into an alleged breach of the code of conduct for police officers (*see also* **Code of Conduct**).

Regulation 13: a reference to the police regulations relating to the dismissal of a probationary police officer.

Reid technique: a technique for interviewing and interrogation developed and used in the US. The technique relies upon the verbal and non-verbal responses to certain preplanned questions, such as 'what should happen to the offender?', which are then analysed by the interviewer to decide if the interviewee is still a suspect or is providing witness evidence. Because the technique can be used to psychologically break down and manipulate a suspect leading them to a confession, this technique of interviewing would not be allowed within the UK criminal justice system (*see also* **Cognitive interview** and **PEACE**).

Release on licence: when an individual serving a custodial sentence for an offence is released early subject to certain conditions. Any breaches of these conditions, such as committing another offence, would mean that the individual would have to return to prison to complete the original custodial sentence.

Remand in custody: a court may remand an individual charged with an offence but not yet convicted to remain in either police or prison custody until a set trial date. Reasons for a remand into custody include the charge of murder or rape and the likelihood that the defendant may interfere with a witness.

Response policing: a reactive law enforcement role with police officers responding to incidents, often using police vehicles, as and when they are reported.

Restricted: it may be undesirable for information containing the word 'restricted' (e.g. some police training manuals) to be revealed to an unauthorized person, as it may prejudice the interests of an individual or the organization (*see also* **Confidential, Disclosure, Secret** and **Top secret**).

Revenue budget: allocation of finances to run the constabulary.

RIDDOR: Reporting of Injuries, Diseases and Dangerous Occurrences Regulations (1995); there is a legal responsibility to report deaths, major injuries, certain diseases and dangerous occurrences to the Health and Safety Executive. Analysis of such incidents and accidents by the Health and Safety Executive (HSE) enables them to identify where and how risks arise which, in turn, may help to reduce injury, ill health and accidents. An example of an incident reportable under RIDDOR is an employee becoming a victim of physical violence that results in an injury (*see also* **HSE**).

Rigor mortis: the stiffness found in muscles within the body shortly after death. Caused by chemical imbalances, rigor mortis is usually found within the muscles of the body approximately four hours after death and starts to leave the body due to the breakdown of muscle fibres after approximately 36 hours. There are however very many factors that can affect these times, such as the condition of clothing, heating, immersion in water, and so on (*see also* **PM**).

Riot: a riot is any urban disorder where a group of 12 or more individuals come together and use or threaten to use violence to achieve a common aim. Riots occurred during the early 1980s in the UK, such as those in Brixton,

London and Toxteth, Liverpool. During a riot in Tottenham, London during 1985, PC Keith Blakelock was murdered; this was the first murder of a police officer in England and Wales during a riot for 152 years (Loader and Mulcahy 2003) (*see also* **Public order training**).

Riot shield: large and small clear polycarbonate shields used by law enforcement agencies to give protection from thrown items (e.g. bottles) and someone hitting out at them when operating in a situation of public disorder or attempting to contain and restrain an individual. Such riot shields are not bullet proof (*see also* **Public order training** and **Riot**).

RIPA: Regulation of Investigatory Powers Act (2000); RIPA legislation was introduced to regulate intrusive surveillance, such as telephone tapping, and the use of human intelligence sources (*see also* **Surveillance**).

RIP(S)A: Regulation of Investigatory Powers (Scotland) Act (2000); as with England and Wales, RIP(S)A legislation was introduced to regulate intrusive surveillance, such as telephone tapping, and the use of human intelligence sources across Scotland (*see also* **Surveillance**).

Risk assessment: a risk assessment deals with identifying safety hazards, assessing the risk involved and recording findings in order to minimize the risk.

RMI form: Racially Motivated Incident form; a form completed by a police officer recording the details of the incident, victim and, if known, the offender.

RMP: Royal Military Police; provides policing and investigative services to all army personnel and establishments around the world (*see* **Appendix 1**).

RM Pol: Royal Marines Police; provides policing and investigative services to all Royal Marine personnel and bases both on land and at sea (*see* **Appendix 1**).

RNP: Royal Navy Police; provides policing and investigative services to all Royal Navy personnel (*see* **Appendix 1**).

Roads Policing Unit: a police unit within each police force staffed by specially trained police drivers who have responsibility for the reduction of casualties on the roads (each year amounting to approximately 3500 deaths and 35 000 serious injuries), enforcing the law on road users, tackling terrorism, dealing with anti-social road use and enhancing public confidence in the police by the use of high-visibility patrols of the roads (ACPO et al. 2005) (*see also* **Bikesafe/Bikewise, Boxing, Pursuit, Rolling block** and **RTC**).

Rohypnol: Rohypnol is the trade name for flunitrazepam, a member of the benzodiazepine family marketed by Roche. It was first synthesized in 1972 and was used in hospitals when deep sedation was needed. It has powerful hypnotic sedative effects and also acts as a muscle relaxant and reduces anxiety. These effects combined with the fact that it can cause amnesia has led to it being used in drug-facilitated sexual assault. Rohypnol takes effect within half an hour of oral administration, and the effects can last for up to 6 hours, with some effects (e.g. amnesia) persisting for up to 12 hours on occasion. This can result in delayed reporting of offences; and since the major metabolite of Rohypnol is only detectable in blood for 12–24 hours or so and in urine for 3–4 days, any delays can lead to the loss of crucial forensic evidence. Although Rohypnol is probably the most well known of the so-called 'date rape' drugs it has not been widely encountered in the UK, with alcohol and other benzodiazepines such as Temazepam being much more common (*see also* **Date rape drugs**).

Rolling block: a technique used by specially trained police drivers to slow traffic on a motorway by placing his or her vehicle in front of vehicles on the carriageway in order to gradually slow down the following vehicles so that, for example, debris can be removed from a carriageway safely, prior to the following vehicles reaching the area of debris (*see also* **Boxing, Pursuit** and **Roads Policing Unit**).

Romeo: a letter of the phonetic alphabet that is utilized to describe the letter R (*see* **Appendix 4**).

RoSPA: Royal Society for the Prevention of Accidents; a charity that provides advice, guidance and training to assist in the reduction of accidents including those on the road, in the water or at home. RoSPA work closely with the police service, particularly in relation to safety on the roads (RoSPA 2008).

RSPB: Royal Society for the Protection of Birds; a charity that looks after the interests of birds and their environment through protection and conservation, educational programmes and law enforcement, usually in collaboration with the police, of those who commit crimes in relation to birds (e.g. stealing rare eggs).

RSPCA: Royal Society for the Prevention of Cruelty to Animals; a charity that looks after the interests of all animals. The RSPCA are known for their protection and rehoming of domestic pets, veterinary services, educational programmes and law enforcement, often by their own Inspectors, in relation to animal abuse, and so on.

RTC: Road traffic collision (previously road traffic accident); described within a good deal of road traffic legislation, the word 'collision' rather than 'accident' is now more accurately used to describe an incident that usually has some contributing factor such as speed (*see also* **Roads Policing Unit**).

RVP: rendezvous point; an easily identifiable location where all the emergency services, and if required later the investigating agencies, can use to assemble vehicles and resources and access to the location can be controlled (*see also* **Scene log**).

R. v.: Regina versus, when a defendant is taken to court by the Crown Prosecution Service acting on behalf of the Crown, the case being heard is said to be Regina (i.e. the Crown) versus the defendant (who would be named). As such some of the paperwork in relation to a particular case (e.g. exhibit labels) would be marked with the information R. v. the defendant's name.

S

SANE: sexual assault nurse examiner (*see* **Forensic nursing**).

SAR: Search and Rescue; traditionally referring to the search and rescue helicopters operated by the Royal Navy, Royal Air Force and Coastguard organization based around the country. SAR also includes the numerous mountain and fell rescue teams with specialist skills that may assist the police (*see also* **MRT**).

SARA: Scanning, Analysis, Response, Assessment; a problem-solving technique that involves the officer scanning for ongoing problems, analysing the problem to attain a better understanding, responding with appropriate policing techniques or wider interagency involvement, and assessing its effectiveness and identifying how things could be improved for the future. The key to the effective use of SARA is the ability of the officer to move backwards and forwards between the stages of the process as required (McLaughlin 2007) (*see also* **Problem-oriented policing**).

SARC: Sexual Assault Referral Centre; the concept of the provision of SARCs has been around since the 1980s when the lack of provision for dealing and caring with survivors of rape and sexual assault was brought to the fore in a now infamous TV 'fly on the wall' documentary 'Police'. The programme was first broadcast in 1982 and documented how poorly an accusation of rape was dealt with by the police. The aim of the modern SARC is to provide a comprehensive and integrated approach to survivors of rape and sexual assault to ensure the best provision of medical care, forensic evidence recovery and personal support. The provision should be in a building away from a police station with restricted access and the availability of interagency care and support, which places the survivor and their needs and wishes as the focus (*see also* **SANE**).

SARDA: Search and Rescue Dog Association; a team of volunteers who operate specially trained search dogs to assist in the location of casualties predominantly within the mountains, moors and fells.

SB: *see* **Special Branch**.

Scarman report: a report into the Brixton riots of 1981 and the tensions that existed between some elements of the black community and the police. The report, which questioned whether institutional racism existed within the police, concluded that there should be a stronger emphasis on community policing, improved training and more recruitment from ethnic minority groups (*see also* **Institutional racism, MacPherson report** and **Swamp 81**).

SCC: Strategic Command Course; a national programme that prepares senior managers within the police service for strategic positions within the service.

SCDEA: Scottish Crime and Drug Enforcement Agency; an organization established at the start of the twenty-first century aimed at preventing and detecting serious and organized crime across Scotland. It is also responsible for liaison with SOCA in England and Wales (*see also* **DEA, Organized crime, SOCA, SPSA, Transnational policing** and **Tulliallan**).

Scene log: a record commenced by the first officer attending a scene of a crime. The scene log should record the details and times that anyone enters and leaves the scene, his or her reason for being there and whether he or she wore protective clothing to prevent contamination (*see also* **RVP**).

Science Policy Unit: a Home Office unit responsible for overseeing the strategic strategies that utilize science and technology and its applications within the police service, such as forensic services and air support units.

Scimitar: Serious Crime Intelligence Management Information Technology and Resources; an intensive course for senior police officers that reflects on lessons learnt from previous serious crimes and provides updates on technology and guidelines for investigations.

Scotland Yard: a small yard behind Whitehall Place in London, around which grew the original Metropolitan Police Headquarters. Scotland Yard is now synonymous with the Metropolitan Police.

SDA: Student development assessor (*see* **Tutor constable**).

SE 1: Street Encounter form; instigated in response to the MacPherson report into the death of Stephen Lawrence. A police officer, special constable or PCSO can issue the Street Encounter form. The process formalizes, records and allows analysis of stop and searches of individuals (*see also* **Stop and search**).

Search: the visual or physical checking of an individual, individual's property, vehicle or premises for people or items (*see also* **Intimate search**).

SEARCH assessment: applicants for employment as a police officer must successfully complete a SEARCH (Structured Entrance Assessment Recruitment Constables Holistically) assessment centre run by the police service where candidates are observed conducting a range of exercises specifically designed to allow them to demonstrate their potential to be effective police officers (*see also* **Job-related fitness test** and **PIRT**).

Search warrant: issued by a magistrate or judge, a search warrant provides a police officer, or other law enforcement practitioner, the legal right to search individuals or property for illegal items (*see also* **Warrant**).

Secret: if information containing the word 'secret' (e.g. anti-terrorism plans) was revealed to an unauthorized person, it would cause serious injury to the interests of that individual, organization or nation (*see also* **Confidential, Disclosure, Restricted** and **Top secret**).

Section 136 Mental Health Act: defined under the Mental Health Act (1983), a police officer can remove a person who appears to be suffering from mental disorder, may be a risk to themselves or others, and requires care or control, from a public place to a safe place, such as a police station or hospital.

Section officer: a rank within the Special Constabulary.

Sector Skills Council: organizations licensed from the government to identify the needs of a particular workforce (e.g. health or policing) and take a lead on driving ahead an enhancement of the required knowledge and skills for effective working within the twenty-first century. The Sector Skills Council for the police service is Skills for Justice (*see also* **NTO** and **Skills for Justice**).

Secured by Design: a scheme managed by the Association of Chief Police Officers that recognizes good practice for designing out crime such as well-lit streets and alleys.

Security Industry Authority: established under the Private Security Industry Act (2001), the Security Industry Authority is responsible for the licensing and managing of those who work in the private security industry such as door supervisors and private investigators (Security Industry Authority 2008).

Seizure: under the Police and Criminal Evidence Act (1984) a police officer may seize (take possession) of anything that may be evidence relating to an offence or to prevent evidence being hidden, lost, changed or destroyed.

Serial killer: an individual who continues to commit murders over a period of time, it is generally accepted that three or more murders by a single person constitutes serial killing (Holmes and Holmes 1998; Schechter and Everitt

2006). An example of a serial killer would be Peter Sutcliffe (infamously known as the Yorkshire Ripper) who in 1981 was found guilty of committing 13 murders and 7 attempted murders between 1975 and 1980 (*see also* **Byford report, Corporate manslaughter, Homicide, Honour killing, Mass murder, Murder/Manslaughter, Murder manual** and **Spree killer**).

Serology: a system for grouping samples of blood using a system of A, B and O.

Sexual offences: a good deal of legislation details offences of a sexual nature such as rape, sexual assault, prostitution, kerb crawling and indecent photographs. The legislation includes the Sexual Offences Act 2003; Criminal Justice Act 1988; Protection of Children Act 1978 and the Street Offences Act 1959 (*see also* **Registered sex offender** and **Sexual Offences Prevention Order**).

Sexual Offences Prevention Order (SOPO): defined within the Sexual Offences Act 2003, a SOPO can be imposed by a court on an individual to help protect the public or particular individual from sexual harm by the person named in the order (*see also* **Registered sex offender** and **Sexual offences**).

SGM+: Second Generation Multiplex plus; a very sensitive method for the examination of recovered DNA samples from a crime scene with specific sites of an individual's DNA.

SGT: Sergeant; a police officer rank.

SHACKS: a mnemonic to assist in deciding if there are reasonable grounds for a stop and search (*see* **Reasonable grounds for suspicion**).

Sheehy inquiry: Sir Patrick Sheehy published a report for the home office in 1993 making a number of recommendations for policing including fixed-term contracts, performance-related pay, changes to allowances for housing/rent and abolition of certain ranks (*see also* **Edmund Davies report**).

Sheriff: with the route of the title of sheriff embedded in history, the contemporary title of sheriff could refer to a local law enforcement officer in the US, a judge in a Scottish Sheriff's Court or a civil appointment by the Crown in England and Wales. Originally the title of shire reeve was bestowed on an individual who had responsibility for overseeing the royal reeves who, in turn, exercised judicial power over a loose group of families. Over time the shire reeve became referred to as the sheriff (Critchley 1967) (*see also* **Sheriff's Court**).

Sheriff's Court: a Scottish Court within the Scottish legal system.

Shoefit: a computerized system that creates databases of footwear images recovered from the scene of a crime, footwear images recovered overtly from people in custody and reference images of known types of footwear (*see also* **Footwear evidence** and **SICAR**).

SIA: *see* **Security Industry Authority**.

SICAR: Shoeprint Image Capture and Retrieval; a computerized system, which creates databases of footwear images, recovered from the scene of a crime, footwear images recovered overtly from people in custody and reference images of known types of footwear. All these databases can be compared with each other (*see also* **Footwear evidence** and **Shoefit**).

SIDS: Sudden infant death syndrome; also known as sudden unexplained death in infancy (SUDI), is the label given to the sudden death of an infant under 18 months of age who previously was thought to be healthy and a post-mortem has failed to find a cause of death.

Sierra: a letter of the phonetic alphabet that is utilized to describe the letter S (*see* **Appendix 4**).

Silver Commander: the commander responsible for the tactical decisions at the scene of an incident, such as the formulation of plans to sustain the level of response to the incident and the support required in order to deal with the incident effectively (e.g. the establishment of a casualty bureau). Also called the tactical commander (*see also* **Bronze commander, Gold commander and Golden hour**).

SIM: Subscriber Identity Module; a card within a mobile telephone containing the telephone number and other encoded network information.

Single non-emergency number: a single national telephone number, 101, which does not replace the emergency 999 number; instead, it should be used by the general public to report incidences that are not an emergency. Incidences reported using 101, such as graffiti, neighbourhood disputes or drug-related anti-social behaviour, will receive advice and guidance over the telephone and sometimes a visit by an appropriate member of the law enforcement community.

SIO: Senior police investigating officer; the police officer, often an experienced detective, who leads and has ultimate responsibility for the investigation of a major crime such as a murder, serial crime or terrorist incident (*see also* **Byford report, CID, Major incident room** and **MIT**).

Situational crime prevention: a crime prevention theory that highlights the importance of the situation presented to the likely offender, which includes the physical environment, but also the opportunities presented, such as the presence of desirable goods and people (*see also* **Architectural liaison officer, CPO** and **Crime prevention through environmental design**).

Skills for Justice: evolved during 2004 from the Police Skills and Standards Organization, Skills for Justice is the National Training Organization and Sector Skills Council for the Police Service with a focus on developing a suite of skills for policing and related occupations (*see* **Appendix 3**) (*see also* **NOS, NTO, Sector Skills Council** and **Skillsmark**).

Skillsmark: a quality mark administered by Skills for Justice that recognizes and approves training and education providers along with the endorsement of specific programmes as being appropriate for the criminal justice sector (*see also* **NOS** and **Skills for Justice**).

SLDP: Senior Leadership Development Programmes; specialist programmes, such as the command of critical incidents, for those law enforcement officers working, or hoping to work, within strategic positions.

SLP: Single locus probe or self-loading pistol; single locus probe is a method for the examination of four specific sites of an individual's DNA. This older method of DNA analysis allowed for the first time mixed blood stains recovered from the crime scene to be differentiated from each other.

A self-loading pistol is a type of handgun that uses some of the energy released when a shot is fired to eject the spent cartridge case and reload the handgun with another round from a magazine.

SMART: Specific, measurable, achievable, realistic, bound by time; a method for planning objectives.

SmartWater: a range of commercial products that can be used to uniquely mark goods (product traditionally known as SmartWater Tracer) or be covertly installed to mark criminals committing offences. Smartwater is only visible under the correct wavelength of ultraviolet light (*see also* **UV**).

SMV: stolen motor vehicle.

SOCA: the Serious Organized Crime Agency was established as a national law enforcement agency in April 2006. The amalgamation of the National Crime Squad (NCS), National Criminal Intelligence Service (NCIS), along with the investigative wing of Her Majesty's Revenue and Customs and immigration investigators, allows this Home Office-sponsored but independent body to focus on intelligence-led law enforcement of organized activities such as drug trafficking, immigration and fraud across the UK (SOCA 2006) (*see also* **Organized crime, Transnational policing** and **SCDEA**).

SOCAP Act: Serious Organized Crime and Police Act (2005); legislation that formed part of the government's police reform agenda. The Serious Organized Crime and Police Act established the Serious Organized Crime Agency (*see also* **SOCA**).

SOCIMS: Scenes of Crime Information and Management System; a commercially produced IT system designed to deal with the tracking of forensic submissions.

SOCKET: a commercially produced IT system designed to track evidence recovered by CSIs from the crime scene.

SOCO: scenes of crime officer (*see* **CSE/CSI**).

SOCRATES: a commercially produced integrated evidence management system for use by a range of forensic practitioners. The system consists of a range of IT modules, such as SOCIMS and SOCKET, each of which are individualized for use by certain types of forensic practitioner.

SOLAP: Student Officer Learning and Development Portfolio; a record of the progress a student officer has made towards completion of his or her National Occupational Standards (NOS) (*see also* **Community placement, Independent patrol, IPLDP, PACS** and **Reflective diary**).

Solcara Crisis Control Centre: a commercial web-based IT package that can be interrogated by nominated individuals to quickly assimilate and disseminate information rapidly.

Solicitor: a legal professional who liaises with the client to prepare the criminal case for court; although solicitors can appear in court, it is common practice for them to instruct barristers to represent them within the court (*see also* **Duty solicitor**).

SOP: standard operating procedure.

SOPO: see **Sexual Offences Prevention Order**.

SORN: Statutory Off Road Notification; the notification completed by the owner of a vehicle to the DVLA that the vehicle in question is not used on the public highway.

SPC: Scottish Police College, based at Tulliallan Castle, Fife, the SPC provides training for the Scottish Police Service.

SPCP: Service Police Codes of Practice (2006); initially derived from the Police and Criminal Evidence Act (1984), SPCP provide guidance as to the key areas of service (military) police procedures relating to stop and search, searching premises and seizing property, treatment and questioning individuals, identification of individuals, audio and visual recording of interviews and powers of arrest. These codes can be found in the joint services publication number 397.

Special Branch: a department within each police force that focuses its investigations into those likely to become involved in subversive activities likely to affect life or property (*see also* **Border agency, Ports officer** and **Terrorism**).

Special constable: the Special Constables Act (1931) allowed magistrates to appoint volunteer unpaid police officers who have the powers of regular officers. There are now over 14 000 special constables across England and Wales, over 1000 special constables in Scotland and colleagues performing similar roles in Northern Ireland.

Special priority post payment: extra payments received by police officers for conducting certain roles within the organization that require, for example, specific technical skills or expose officers to an increased risk of serious assault.

SPR: small particle reagent; a forensic method that uses a suspension to develop fingerprints on non-porous surfaces such as polythene bags.

Spree killer: an individual who suddenly goes on a spree of murder killing everyone who fits a particular profile, such as female or living in a particular location, until they are caught or stopped. An example of a spree killer is Michael Ryan who in 1987 went on a spree of murder with a range of firearms in Hungerford resulting in the deaths of 16 people (*see also* **Corporate manslaughter, Homicide, Honour killing, Mass murder, Murder/Manslaughter, Murder manual** and **Serial killer**).

SPSA: Scottish Police Services Authority; established in 2007 the SPSA encompasses and centralizes the specialist expertise of Scottish organizations, such as the Scottish Police College at Tulliallan, Forensic Services, Scottish Crime and Drug Enforcement Agency and Information collation and dissemination in support of the eight police forces across Scotland (Scottish Police Services Authority 2008) (*see also* **SCDEA, SPC** and **Tulliallan**).

SSAT: Stop and Search Action Team; established by the government in 2006, the SSAT is headed by two ministers of state and aims to ensure that stop and search powers are used both fairly and effectively by the police as a tool in the prevention and detection of crime (*see also* **Stop and search**).

SSC: scientific support coordinator (*see also* **CSC**) is usually a senior crime scene manager. The SSC is responsible for the strategic coordination of the forensic investigation of a number of linked crime scenes.

SSM: scientific support manager; the SSM has overall management of scientific and forensic resources, such as photography, crime scene investigation, fingerprint bureau, fingerprint development laboratory and plan drawing within a police force. Either a senior police officer or civilian member of staff the SSM also acts as the chief adviser on forensic matters to the force.

SSU: Scientific Services Unit; the police department usually encompassing photographic, crime scene investigation, fingerprint comparison, fingerprint development, plan drawing and sometimes technical support services to the force.

Statement: a written record of an individual's involvement in an incident or occurrence, usually written on an MG11 form (*see* **Appendix 2**).

Statement taker: a civilian role with law enforcement solely trained to interview and record in the form of a statement information from victims and witnesses.

Stinger: a commercial device used by trained police officers throughout the UK and the US to halt vehicles fleeing from pursuit. The device consists of a series of spikes attached to a concertinaed bed that can be flung across a road in the path of a fleeing vehicle. The vehicle tyres are punctured and will gradually deflate bringing the vehicle to a halt; the device can immediately be retracted to ensure there is no damage to the following vehicles.

Stop and search: defined under PACE 1984, a police officer, and in some forces community support officers are also authorized under specific legislation, can stop and search any person or vehicle if they believe that they will find drugs, weapons, and so on; the details of the stop and search must be recorded by the officer. However, research has shown that the success rates for stop and search uncovering an offence can be as low as one stop in ten, yet the resultant alienation of a community against the police can be high (Reiner 2000) (*see also* **GOWISELY, SE 1, SSAT** and **Swamp 81**).

STR: Short tandem repeats (STRs) form part of the DNA molecule. The DNA molecule resembles a long spiralling ladder, the two sides of which are made up of building blocks called nucleotides. Each nucleotide is made of a sugar joined to a phosphate and a base. The bases come in four varieties – A (adenosine), C (cytosine), G (guanine) and T (thiamine), and it is the order that these bases appear in along the DNA ladder that makes up our genetic code. The bases pair up according to strict rules – A only ever pairs with T, and C only ever pairs with G. The A–T and C–G base pairs, repeated in various sequences make up the three billion 'rungs' of the DNA ladder. In some parts of the DNA molecule, known as polymorphic regions, short bursts of repeated sequences, 3–20 base pairs long, repeated over and over appear. These repeated sections, known as STRs, have no known function, but they vary markedly between individuals, so are used to make up the DNA profile used for crime fighting purposes (*see also* **DNA**).

Street warden: *see* **Crime warden**.

Structured debrief: structured debriefing is a tool for reviewing experiences. Introduced by the Centre for Structured Debriefing in 1994, it is widely used in the public, private and voluntary sectors to monitor and develop performance. In policing it is often used to review operational incidents. It is a disciplined but flexible technique for learning through reflection by sharing experiences, gathering information, and developing ideas for the future.

Subpoena: a summons issued by the court requiring the attendance of a witness to give evidence within the court.

Sudden death: an unexpected and unexplained death.

Summary offence: One of three classifications of criminal offences. A summary offence (e.g. common assault, criminal damage or drunk and disorderly) is heard and dealt with in a Magistrates Court (Hannibal and Mountford 2002). Although in certain circumstances a summary offence can be heard within a Crown Court, when it is felt by the magistrates that the case would be better dealt with by a trial by jury or there is the possibility that a sentence may be required that is greater than that which magistrates can impose (*see also* **Either way offence** and **Indictable Offence**).

Superglue: a forensic method that uses superglue vapours to develop fingerprints on non-porous surfaces.

SUPT: superintendent; a police officer rank.

Surveillance: gathering information by a range of covert and overt methods ranging from photographic and CCTV images to the use of electronic listening devices in order to manage people, places or inanimate objects (*see also* **CCTV** and **RIPA**).

SVS: Stolen Vehicle Squad; a department within each police force whose staff have specialist skills in the investigation of crimes involving the theft, tampering with and resale of motor vehicles and vehicle parts (*see also* **AVCIS**).

Swamp 81: a large-scale stop and search policing operation conducted by the Metropolitan Police within the Brixton area during early 1981. The operation resulted in ever increasing tension between the community and the police and in April 1981 resulted in the Brixton riots (*see also* **Scarman report** and **Stop and search**).

SWAT: Special Weapons and Tactics; a common police unit across the US that specializes in dealing with dangerous and armed operations (*see also* **Tactical Firearms Unit**).

SYP: South Yorkshire Police (*see* **Appendix 1**).

T

Tactical Firearms Unit: a unit of police officers within each force specially trained to carry firearms to respond to, contain and deal with incidents involving firearms (*see also* **AFO, ARV, Firearm** and **SWAT**).

TAG: Tactical Aid Group, police officers specially trained to conduct searches.

TAM: terrorism and allied matters; a generic term (*see also* **CT** and **Terrorism**).

Tamper evident bag: a polythene bag used for the packaging of items recovered from crime scenes and suspects, which after sealing shows a marker if someone attempts to tear open the seal of the bag (often displaying words such as void within the seal).

Tango: a letter of the phonetic alphabet that is utilized to describe the letter T (*see* **Appendix 4**).

Target hardening: making premises less likely to fall victim of a crime due to the addition of measures, such as better locks, alarms and fences.

Task force: a police unit made up of specially trained officers providing support services to operational policing, such as search teams, surveillance operations, counter terrorism and public disorder.

Taser: a less than lethal weapon that looks like a pistol but fires two barbs into the individual, which then stuns him or her, using a short burst of electricity amounting to some 50 000 volts. Since the first trials of their use in the UK during 2003, the Taser, named after its designer in the 1970s, the T.A. Swift electrical rifle (Rogers 2003) can only be used by specially trained and authorized officers on individuals demonstrating violent or threatening behaviour (*see also* **Baton round**).

TDA: taking and driving away; an outdated term, which has now been superseded by TWOC, for the theft of a motor vehicle (*see* **TWOC**).

TDO: training and development officer; specially trained police officers who provide individual coaching, learning and assessment for police officers.

Temazepam: a tranquillizer from the benzodiazepine family that can be prescribed for medical use; however, it is often abused by drug users. It depresses alertness and when taken in high doses can cause drowsiness and sleep. It is used by some heroin addicts as a means to maintain their equilibrium until they can get their next 'fix' of heroin. Temazepam's soporific effects have also led to it being utilized as a date rape drug.

Tenprints: inked or computer-scanned images of the 10 fingers and palms of an individual that can be compared by experts with fingerprints or palmprints recovered from the scene of a crime (*see also* **Fingerprints**).

Terrorism: usually deemed to be the planned use, or threat of use, of serious violence, or the extreme fear of violence, to influence government (regionally, nationally or internationally), a particular section of the community or an organization. However, there is no one definition of terrorism that can be applied to every occurrence; instead, being covered by a good deal of contemporary legislation including the Terrorism Act 2000, Anti-terrorism, Crime and Security Act 2001, the Prevention of Terrorism Act 2005 and the Terrorism Act 2006 (Home Office 2007b; Walker 2006). Since the attacks on the New York World Trade Center on 11 September 2001, the general public have become acutely aware of the potential consequences of terrorist acts, yet in the UK the authorities have been responding to terrorism for many years from the ex-colonial countries, such as Kenya and Malaysia to closer at home in Northern Ireland and mainland Britain (Walker 2006). From 11 September 2001 until 31 March 2007 the Home Office reports that, excluding Northern Ireland, 1228 people were arrested under the existing terrorist legislation (Home Office 2007b). The legislation is constantly being reviewed and updated; for example, the Terrorism Act 2006 introduced offences relating to the preparation for terrorist activity or the encouragement of terrorist acts (*see also* **CT, CTSA, CTU, JTAC, NaCTSO, Special Branch** and **TAM**).

Test purchase: a specially trained and authorized police officer can act as a buyer to purchase illegal goods such as drugs.

TFU: Tactical Firearms Unit; the police unit that provides specially trained and equipped 24-hour 365-days-a-year firearms support (e.g. armed response vehicles) to the police service. TFU are known as SO19 in the Metropolitan Police Service (*see also* **ARV**).

Theft: defined within the Theft Act 1968, a theft occurs when someone appropriates property that belongs to another person with no intention of returning it.

TI: trainee investigator (*see also* **CID, Designated investigator, ICIDP, IO, MIT** and **SIO**).

TIC: taken into consideration; an offence admitted by a defendant for which they have not been charged.

TLC: thin layer chromatography; a forensic laboratory technique that can be used to separate out the active ingredients in drugs (e.g. cannabis).

TNA: training needs analysis; a process usually conducted independently that reviews the learning needs of individuals and the occupational role they perform or are required to perform and then embeds these in the learning needs of the department in which they work and the organization's needs and aspirations.

Top secret: if information containing the words 'top secret' was revealed to an unauthorized person, it would cause grave damage to the interests of that individual, organization or nation (*see also* **Confidential, Disclosure, Restricted** and **Secret**).

Toxicology: toxicology is concerned with the study on a scientific basis of both drugs and poisons (Langford et al. 2005) (*see also* **Forensic toxicology**).

Trace forensic evidence: usually held to be small amounts of physical forensic evidence (e.g. glass, paint, hairs or fibres) that may require microscopic examination but may link, for example, suspects to crime scenes.

Tracker: a commercial tracking system hidden within a vehicle that when activated allows the stolen vehicle to be tracked and recovered by the law enforcement agencies.

Trading Standards: a national organization which, through enforcement officers employed in local offices, protects the public by means of persuasion and if necessary prosecutions relating to, for example, the safety of products, food irregularities and counterfeited goods.

Transnational policing: policing activity that extends beyond the more traditional borders and boundaries and includes law enforcement in relation to the interchange of commercial activity (e.g. the supply of internal security equipment to another state's police), the migration of people (e.g. police liaison officers working within Europe and beyond) and ideas (e.g. intellectual property being stolen via the internet) (Sheptycki 2000) (*see also* **Europol, Interpol, Organized crime, SCDEA** and **SOCA**).

TreadMark: a forensic computerized footwear comparison system used to analyse and identify footwear marks.

Trident, Operation: a Metropolitan Police operation established in the late 1990s targeting the reduction of firearms crime among the young black community (Metropolitan Police Authority 2007).

TRL&DP: Training Roles Learning & Development Programme; a modular programme of learning and development that allows police students to study at a pace appropriate for them to achieve the differing roles related to training, learning and development (e.g. presenter and instructor) required by the police service.

Truncheon: originally used as a symbol of authority, police issue truncheons are now outdated in preference to ASPs and batons but were used by a police officer for his or her defence (*see also* **ASP** and **Baton**).

TSU: technical support unit; TSUs consist of skilled technicians who gather evidence in relation to organized crime and provide related support to a police force. This includes gathering, often in a covert environment, video, audio, photographic and other sensitive evidence and intelligence in a lawful manner.

Tulliallan: Scottish Police College, based around Tulliallan castle, has provided training and education to the Scottish Police Service since the 1950s (*see also* **SPC** and **SPSA**).

Turnbull Rule: the outcome of the case of *R. v. Turnbull* and others (1977) led to the direction that a judge should warn a jury to be cautious when convicting on identification evidence, such as that of an eyewitness, as a whole range of factors may influence the recall of a witness (*see also* **ADVOKATE**).

Tutor constable: experienced police officers who receive specialist training to enable them to coach and mentor new probationary police officers during their early exposure to the operational police environment (*see also* **PDU** and **SDA**).

TVP: Thames Valley Police (*see* **Appendix 1**).

TW: traffic warden; a role responsible for monitoring controlled and restricted parking areas, identifying infringements within such areas and issuing fixed penalty notices.

TWLA: taking a motor vehicle without lawful authority (*see* **TWOC**).

TWOC: taking a motor vehicle without the owner's consent. Defined within the Theft Act 1968, this is when an individual is temporarily deprived of his or her motor vehicle without first giving their permission.

U

UHF: ultra high-frequency communication systems used in radio transmission.

UN: United Nations; established by a charter signed in New York by the member states in 1945, the United Nations aims to ensure international peace and security, foster international relations in respect of economies, social, cultural and humanitarian needs. The UN plays a significant role in the evolution of international law and justice, such as the provision of assistance in the ratification and embedding of legal instruments in countries in order to, for example, counter terrorism or coordinate activities to tackle crimes against vulnerable groups (United Nations 2004).

Underwater Search Unit: police officers specially trained in the use of sub-aqua equipment to search for and recover evidence, such as bodies, cars and firearms or to ensure that areas are clear from terrorist devices. The underwater search unit can operate in water features, such as canals, ponds and rivers, along with confined spaces requiring self-contained breathing apparatus, such as sewers.

Uniform: a letter of the phonetic alphabet that is utilized to describe the letter U (*see* **Appendix 4**), and the identifiable types of clothes worn by members of the same organization.

Unison: trade union that represents the needs in relation to pay and employment rights of well over one million public service employees working in areas as diverse as the NHS, schools and the water supply industry. Unison also represents the interests of over 40 000 civilian staff who work within the police service (Unison 2007) (*see also* **Police Federation**).

URN: unique reference number; the issue by the police of a URN is usually associated with the aim to reduce the need for a police response to false activations of intruder alarms. When an appropriately installed alarm that meets industry standards is installed and monitored by a receiving centre, the fact that the alarm system has been issued with a URN ensures its reliability, so when it activates the monitoring centre will inform the police who will respond as soon as possible to the scene of the activation (*see also* **Levels of police response to intruder alarms**).

Use of force: any law enforcement officer using force while performing his or her lawful duty (ranging from making an arrest to shooting an individual) must be able to demonstrate that the force used adheres to the mnemonic PLAN; that is, the force was **P**roportionate to the situation, had **L**egality under the law, the officer must be able to **A**ccount for the actions they took and the actions they did not take and be able to demonstrate that the actions were Necessary to complete their duties.

Usher: a court official, an usher calls witnesses into a court of law and hands around exhibits, and so on as required. It is imperative to let the usher know when a witness has arrived at court (*see also* **Clerk to the court**).

UV: Ultraviolet; a wavelength of light that is within the electromagnetic spectrum but is beyond that which is visible, UV lights are predominantly used by law enforcement to check people and products for SmartWater (*see also* **Smartwater**).

V

VASCAR: visual average speed camera and recorder; a piece of equipment that is used by a police officer to calculate the average speed of a moving vehicle between two points. To use the system an officer must first set the distance to be measured against two fixed points (these could be a bridge, post or marker painted onto the road). When the vehicle passes the first of the markers a button must be pressed, and then again when the vehicle passes the second marker; an average speed will then be calculated. The VASCAR machines should be regularly calibrated to ensure accuracy of use.

VCSI: volume crime scene investigator; a CSI who deals predominantly with the forensic examinations of volume crime scenes (e.g. thefts from vehicles) to recover photographic, forensic and fingerprint evidence (*see also* **CSE/ CSI**).

VDRS: Vehicle Defect Rectification Scheme; a method by which officers can provide the opportunity for motorists to rectify minor problems with their vehicles (e.g. a faulty light) as an alternative to a prosecution.

VDRS Notice: Vehicle Defect Rectification Scheme Notice; a police officer can issue a ticket to the driver of a vehicle with a minor defect for its rectification within a set time period.

Vehicle online descriptive search: part of the Police National Computer, the description of a vehicle's and/or part registration can be searched online in order to identify the vehicle and its registered owner (Povey 2000) (*see also* **Phoenix** and **PNC**).

VEL: vehicle excise licence; issued by the Driver and Vehicle Licensing agency, any mechanically propelled vehicle is required to display a current VEL. However, there are some exemptions such as ambulances and fire engines.

VHF: very high-frequency radio.

VICAP: Violent Crime Apprehension System; A US IT system operated by the FBI that uses a range of data to analyse patterns and trace travelling criminals involved in offences of violent crime (Adderley and Musgrove 2001).

Victimology: with its origins in criminological studies in the 1940s, victimology is the interdisciplinary study of the relationship and interactions between the victim, the offender, the criminal justice system and society as a whole in an effort to identify why things happened and how things could be done differently (Karmen 2007).

Victim Support Scheme: a charity that operates across the UK and Ireland providing information, confidential support and guidance to victims of crime and others affected by crime. The victim support witness service will also assist those attending court (Victim Support Scheme 2008).

Victor: a letter of the phonetic alphabet that is utilized to describe the letter V (*see* **Appendix 4**).

VIN: vehicle identification number; a series of digits (usually 17) stamped into a metal plate attached to the driver's door sill. The number is given to the vehicle during its manufacture and is unique thus allowing the history of the vehicle to be traced via PNC. The numbers can also be interpreted to provide information such as year of manufacture, make of vehicle, and so on (*see also* **Chassis number, Engine number** and **VRM**).

VIP: very important person; an individual deemed by the organization to be a person of high importance (e.g. a member of government or a diplomat).

VIPER: Video Identification Parade Electronic Recording; a computerized database of suspects recorded on a short section of video while they are in custody that can later be shown, with images of individuals with similar physical characteristics, to witnesses of a particular offence (*see also* **Identification parade**).

ViSOR: Violent Sex Offenders Register; a national computer database containing information on convicted sex offenders and their places of residence (*see also* **Protection of Vulnerable Adults Scheme**).

Volunteers in Policing: a national project established to recruit volunteers to work a few hours a week with the police to support them in non-operational roles within the community where the volunteer lives or works.

VOSA: the Vehicle and Operator Services Agency; established in 2003, VOSA conducts a range of activities revolving around the improvement of vehicle roadworthiness and compliance with road traffic legislation. This includes vehicle licensing, testing and enforcement of standards.

VRM: vehicle registration mark; the characters that appear on a number plate displayed on the front and rear of a vehicle is the VRM (DVLA 2007). Originally instigated as a means of unique vehicle registration and recognition in the early 1900s, the VRM has mandatory set sizes and fonts for the characters on vehicle number plates dependent on the age and type of motor vehicle (*see also* **Chassis number, Engine number** and **VIN**).

Vulnerable witness: this includes children under the age of 17, those who have a mental or physical disorder affecting their ability to give evidence, and those who may be distressed by giving such evidence.

W

Warrant: when sworn in as a police constable, the constable is given the authority by a magistrate, or warranted, to take away the liberty of a citizen in order to pursue the interests of law enforcement (*see also* **Search warrant**).

Watson: an IT suite of investigative software used for managing cases and intelligence analysis. As a result of the sharing and interrogation of information, tasks can be prioritized, resources deployed and new lines of enquiry identified (Adderley and Musgrove 2001) (*see also* **Crime pattern analysis, Five × five intelligence, Intelligence, Intelligence analyst, Intelligence cycle** and **NIM**).

Whisky: a letter of the phonetic alphabet that is utilized to describe the letter W (*see* **Appendix 4**).

White collar crime: a criminological term first adopted in the 1930s and used predominantly to refer to offences committed by executives involving business and occupations such as corporate crime, financial crime and fraud (Blount 2002). However, in the contemporary workplace such 'white collar crimes' are no longer limited to executives; instead, they can be committed by anyone within an organization. Such crimes are not easily identified by the organization and are expensive and protracted to investigate (ibid.). An example of a 'white collar crime' was that committed by the rogue trader, Nick Leeson, who as an employee of Barings Bank in Singapore during the early 1990s fraudulently hid the bank's losses of millions of pounds over a period of years before it was discovered. He was arrested and convicted of fraud for which he was imprisoned.

White powder: a white-coloured granular powder used by CSIs to locate fingerprints.

Whorl: a pattern made up of the ridges found on a thumb or finger (*see also* **Fingerprints**).

Wider police family: across the UK the forces that form the contemporary police service combine to employ around 160 000 police officers, 70 000 civilian staff in a range of roles from administrator to CSI, 25 000 police community support officers, 13 000 special constables and other volunteers such as the neighbourhood watch, who together constitute the wider police family.

Wildlife crime officer: a role within the police service that concentrates on the protection, prevention and detection of crime in relation to wild and rare species of wildlife.

Witness: a person who may have information pertaining to the matter in hand.

Witness statement: information taken from the witness and written down (*see also* **ADVOKATE**).

WMP: West Midlands Police (*see* **Appendix 1**).

Wounding: defined under section 18 of the Offences Against the Person Act (1861), a wounding occurs when someone intends to wound or cause grievous bodily harm either by direct action or as a result of their actions.

WRVS: Women's Royal Volunteer Service; a large organization with over 60 000 volunteers and a number of employees who together aim to help those in need, such as the provision of refreshments to the emergency services while dealing with emergency situations, becoming a friend to a lonely person or liaising with other organizations and charities (WRVS 2007).

WYP: West Yorkshire Police (*see* **Appendix 1**).

X

X chromosome: gender-determining chromosomes that are inherited from a male or female. If both chromosomes are X then the resultant offspring will be female.

X-ray: a letter of the phonetic alphabet that is utilized to describe the letter X (*see* **Appendix 4**).

X-ray fluorescence: a technique for laboratory-based high-powered microscopic analysis of forensic samples, such as paint fragments, gunshot residue and fingerprints.

Y

Yankee: a letter of the phonetic alphabet that is utilized to describe the letter Y (*see* **Appendix 4**).

Y chromosome: gender-determining chromosome that are inherited from a male. Inheriting a Y chromosome will result in a male offspring.

YJB: Youth Justice Board; established in 1998 to oversee and give direction to youth offending teams across England and Wales.

YMCA: Young Men's Christian Association; the YMCA can provide housing, training and community support to young people across the UK.

Young person: for the purposes of policing a young person is generally deemed to be a person who has reached the age of 14 but not yet 18 years.

Youth Court: similar to a Magistrates Court, a Youth Court is held in private and adapted to deal with cases against young persons aged 10 to 17 years. There are some exceptions to trials being held in Youth Courts, such as those for murder or where they have been charged jointly with an adult, and in the interests of justice all defendants should be sent for trial.

Youth offending team: made up of representatives from the police, probation service, social services, housing officers, and so on, youth offending teams aim to address the need of each young offender in order to prevent reoffending (*see also* **PYO**).

Z

Zephyr brush: brush used by crime scene investigators when fingerprinting a crime scene. It is used for the application of flake fingerprint powders.

Zero tolerance: a policing philosophy where offences are prosecuted regardless of the type of offence. There is no discretion for those enforcing the law to provide advice for minor misdemeanours or deviant behaviour. With its origins in New York, Burke (1998) suggests that zero tolerance has been accepted more as a philosophy across England and Wales than in the US (*see also* **Broken windows**).

Zulu: a letter of the phonetic alphabet that is utilized to describe the letter Z (*see* **Appendix 4**).

Table of statutes

Anti-terrorism, Crime and Security Act (2001)
Contempt of Court Act (1981)
Corporate Manslaughter and Corporate Homicide Act (2007)
County Courts Act (1888)
Crime and Disorder Act (1998)
Criminal Damage Act (1971)
Criminal Justice Act (1967)
Criminal Justice Act (1988)
Criminal Justice Act (2003)
Criminal Justices and Court Services Act (2000)
Criminal Justice and Police Act (2001)
Criminal Justice and Public Order Act (1994)
Criminal Procedures and Investigation Act (1996)
Data Protection Act (1998)
Disability Discrimination Act (2005)
Domestic Violence, Crime and Victims Act (2004)
Drugs Act (2005)
Employment Rights Act (1996)
Equal Pay Act (1970)
Firearms Act (1968)
Firearms (Amendment) Act (1997)
Football (Offences and Disorder) Act (1999)
Football Spectators Act (1989)
Fraud Act (2006)
Freedom of Information Act (2000)
Gin Act (1736)
Health and Safety at Work Act (1974)
Human Rights Act (1998)
Licensing Act (1872)
Licensing Act (2003)
Metropolitan Police Act (1829)
Offences Against the Person Act (1861)
Perjury Act (1911)
Police and Criminal Evidence Act (1984)
Police (Amendment) Regulations (2005)
Police Reform Act (2002)

Prevention of Crime Act (1953)
Prevention of Terrorism Act (2006)
Private Security Industry Act (2001)
Proceeds of Crime Act (2002)
Prosecution of Offences Act (1985)
Protection of Children Act (1978)
Race Relations Act (1976)
Railways and Transport Safety Act (2003)
Regulation of Investigatory Powers Act (2000)
Regulation of Investigatory Powers (Scotland) Act (2000)
Road Traffic Act (1988)
Rural Constabulary Act (1839)
Serious Organized Crime and Police Act (2005)
Sex Discrimination Act (1975)
Sexual Offences Act (2003)
Sex Offenders Act (1997)
Special Constables Act (1931)
Street Offences Act (1959)
Terrorism Act (2000)
Theft Act (1968)
Traffic Management Act (2004)
UK Borders Act (2007)

Appendix 1: Police forces across the UK

Police forces across England and Wales
(also referred to as Home Office police forces)

Avon and Somerset Constabulary
Bedfordshire Police
Cambridgeshire Constabulary
Cheshire Constabulary
City of London Police
Cleveland Police
Cumbria Constabulary
Derbyshire Constabulary
Devon and Cornwall Constabulary
Dorset Police
Durham Constabulary
Dyfed-Powys Police
Essex Police
Gloucestershire Constabulary
Greater Manchester Police
Gwent Police
Hampshire Constabulary
Hertfordshire Constabulary
Humberside Police
Kent Police
Lancashire Constabulary
Leicestershire Constabulary
Lincolnshire Police
Merseyside Police
Metropolitan Police
Norfolk Constabulary
North Wales Police
North Yorkshire Police
Northamptonshire Police
Northumbria Police
Nottinghamshire Police
South Wales Police
South Yorkshire Police

Staffordshire Police
Suffolk Constabulary
Surrey Police
Sussex Police
Thames Valley Police
Warwickshire Police
West Mercia Constabulary
West Midlands Police
West Yorkshire Police
Wiltshire Constabulary

Police forces across Scotland

Central Scotland Police
Dumfries and Galloway Constabulary
Fife Constabulary
Grampian Police
Lothian and Borders Police
Northern Constabulary
Strathclyde Police
Tayside Police

Northern Ireland

Police Service of Northern Ireland (PSNI)

Non-Home Office police forces

British Transport Police
Civil Nuclear Constabulary
Guernsey Police
Isle of Man Constabulary
Ministry of Defence Police
States of Jersey Police

Belfast Harbour Police
Belfast International Airport Constabulary
Falmouth Docks Police
Larne Harbour Police
Mersey Tunnel Police
Port of Bristol Police
Port of Dover Police
Port of Felixstowe Security and Police

Port of Liverpool Police
Port of Tees and Hartlepool Police
Port of Tilbury Police

Royal Parks Constabulary

Royal Air Force Police
Royal Marines Police
Royal Military Police
Royal Navy Police

Overseas UK police forces

Royal Falkland Islands Police
Royal Gibraltar Police
Sovereign Base Areas Police, Cyprus

Appendix 2: MG forms

MG1	Case file front sheet
MG2	Initial assessment of a witness
MG3	A charging decision report submitted to the Crown Prosecutor. A supplementary form is available for further reports*
MG4	Charge sheet. Supplementary forms are available for specific bail conditions and surety
MG5	Case file summary
MG6	Case file information. Supplementary forms are available to disclose disciplinary records, unused material, sensitive material and as a disclosure report*
MG7	An application for remand
MG8	Breach of the bail conditions
MG9	Witness list
MG10	Witness non-availability
MG11	Statements from witnesses
MG12	Exhibits list and copies of key exhibits
MG13	Application for order on conviction
MG15	Record of interview
MG18	Offences taken into consideration*
MG19	Compensation form
MG20	Further information report
MGFSP	Submission of evidence for forensic examination*
MGNFA	No Further Action*

*(Home Office 2006b)

Appendix 3: National Occupational Standards

Please note that due to the dynamic nature of policing National Occupational Standards are constantly being reviewed and updated to reflect the needs of contemporary law enforcement. Please check the Skills for Justice website (http://www.skillsforjustice.com/) for the most current standards.

National Occupational Standards for Police Officers developed in 2002/2003 (Skills for Justice 2008)

Unit:	Occupational Unit Title
1A1:	Use police actions in a fair and justified way
1A2:	Communicate effectively with members of communities
1A4:	Foster people's equality, diversity and rights
1B9:	Provide initial support to individuals affected by offending or anti-social behaviour and assesses the needs for further support
2A1:	Gather and submit information that has the potential to support policing objectives
2C1:	Provide an initial police response to incidents
2C2:	Prepare for and participate in planned policing operations
2C3:	Arrest, detain or report individuals
2C4:	Minimize and deal with aggressive and abusive behaviour
2G2:	Conduct investigations
2G4:	Finalize investigations
2H1:	Interview victims and witnesses
2H2:	Interview suspects
2I1:	Search individuals
2I2:	Search vehicles, premises and land
2J1:	Prepare and submit case files
2J2:	Present evidence in court and at other hearings
2K1:	Escort detained persons
2K2:	Present detained persons to custody
4C1:	Develop your own knowledge and practice
4G2:	Ensure your own actions reduce risks to health and safety
4G4:	Administer first aid

Revised National Occupational Standards for Policing and Law Enforcement launched in 2008 in order to complement the existing NOS, with the first registrations expected during 2009

Unit:	Occupational Unit Title
CA1:	Use law enforcement actions in a fair and justified way
CB1:	Gather and submit information that has the potential to support law enforcement objectives
CB2:	Evaluate information to determine its intelligence potential
CB3:	Conduct intelligence-driven briefing, tasking and debriefing
CC2:	Formulate, monitor and review tactics to achieve strategic objectives for law enforcement operations
CC3:	Plan and deploy resources for law enforcement operations
CC4:	Determine and review authorizations
CC5:	Identify and manage operational threats and risks
CC6:	Prepare for, monitor and maintain law enforcement operations
CD1:	Provide an initial response to incidents
CD3:	Prepare for, and participate in, planned law enforcement operations
CD5:	Arrest, detain or report individuals
GC10:	Manage conflict
CK1:	Search individuals
CK2:	Search vehicles, premises and open spaces
DA6:	Prepare and submit case files
DA5:	Present evidence in court and at other hearings
GC11:	Respond to allegations or suspicions of child abuse
AA1:	Promote equality and value diversity
AB1:	Communicate effectively with people
AC1:	Contribute to the quality of team working
AD2:	Develop, sustain and evaluate joint work between agencies
AD3:	Represent one's own agency at other agencies' meetings
AE1:	Maintain and develop your own knowledge, skills and competence
AF1:	Ensure your own actions reduce risks to health and safety
AF3:	Promote a health and safety culture within the workplace
AF4:	Conduct an assessment of risk in the workplace
BE2:	Provide initial support to victims, survivors and witnesses and assess their needs for further support
HB11:	Promote equality of opportunity and diversity in your area of responsibility
HD1:	Develop productive working relationships with colleagues
HD11:	Chair and participate in meetings

HE10:   Assess, negotiate and secure sources of funding
HF15:   Provide information to support decision making
HG2:   Establish, maintain and use relationships with the media to explain and promote the agency and its work
HG3:   Support others to make the best use of the media
HG4:   Develop and manage multi-agency partnerships
ZD1:   Develop a strategy and plan for recruitment and selection
ZE1:   Contribute to the development of the knowledge and practice of others

Appendix 4: The phonetic alphabet

A	Alpha
B	Bravo
C	Charlie
D	Delta
E	Echo
F	Foxtrot
G	Golf
H	Hotel
I	India
J	Juliet
K	Kilo
L	Lima
M	Mike
N	November
O	Oscar
P	Papa
Q	Quebec
R	Romeo
S	Sierra
T	Tango
U	Uniform
V	Victor
W	Whisky
X	X-ray
Y	Yankee
Z	Zulu

References

AAIB (2006) *Air Accidents Investigation Branch* (www.aaib.gov.uk: accessed 21 December 2006).

ACPO (2000) *Identifying and combating hate crime*. London: Association of Chief Police Officers.

ACPO (2007a) *Substance Misuse and Testing – Guidance Document*. London: Association of Chief Police Officers.

ACPO (2007b) *Practice Advice on the Policing of Roads*. Bedfordshire: NPIA.

ACPO, Department for Transport & Home Office (2005) *Roads Policing Strategy*. London: ACPO.

ACPO Vehicle Crime Intelligence Service (2008) *About AVCIS* (www.acpo.police.uk/avcis: accessed 11 July 2008).

Adamo, K., McCrum, R. and Gerber. S. (2008) Who owns the patents covering a company's technology? *Intellectual Property & Technology Law Journal*, 20(1): 6–10.

Adderley, R. and Musgrove, P. (2001) Police crime recording and investigation systems: a user's view, *Policing: An International Journal of Police Strategies and Management*, 24(1): 100–14.

Association of Chief Police Officers/Forensic Science Service (1996) *Using Forensic Science Effectively*. Birmingham: ACPO/FSS.

Blount, E. (2002) *Occupational Crime: Deterrence, Investigation, and Reporting in Compliance with Federal Guidelines*. Boca Raton: CRC Press.

Brown, B. (1995) *CCTV in Town Centres: Three Case Studies*. Police Research Group. Crime Detection and Prevention Series 68.

Bullock. K. & Jamieson, I. (1998) The effectiveness of personal development planning. *The Curriculum Journal* 9(1): 63–77.

Bullock, K. and Jones, B (2004) *Acceptable Behaviour Contracts addressing anti-social behaviour in the London Borough of Islington*. Home Office Report 02/04. London: Research and Development Statistics Directorate.

Burke, H. (ed.) (1998) *Zero Tolerance Policing*. Leicester: Perpetuity Press.

Crampton, J., Paterson, K., Piper, F. and Robshaw, M. (2006) Information security, in M. Gill (ed.) *The Handbook of Security*. Hampshire: Palgrave Macmillan.

Crawford, A., Lister, S., Blackburn, S. and Burnett, J. (2005) *Plural Policing: The Mixed Economy of Visible Patrols in England and Wales*. Bristol: Policy Press.

CRB (2007) *Criminal Records Bureau* (www.crb.gov.uk: accessed 18 April 2007).

Critchley, T.A. (1967) *A History of Police in England and Wales 900–1966*. London: Constable and Company.

Crow, D., Form, A., Fraser, G., Giles, T. and Wynn, G. (2006) *Practical Policing Skills for Student Officers*. Exeter: Law Matters Publishing.

Dando, C., Wilcock, R. and Milne, R. (2008) The cognitive interview: inexperienced police officers' perceptions of their witness/victim interviewing practices, *Legal and Criminological Psychology*, 13, 59–70.

Decodts, M. (2005) *Juvenile Reconviction in Northern Ireland 2001*. Belfast: Northern Ireland Office Research and Statistical Bulletin 6.

DEFRA (2007) Department for the Environment, Food and Rural Affairs (www.defra.gov.uk: accessed 21 September 2007).

Dobrin, A. (2006) Professional and community orientated policing: the Mayberry model, *Journal of Criminal Justice and Popular Culture*, 13(1): 19–28.

Downes, D. and Rock, P. (1998) *Understanding Deviance: A Guide to the Sociology of Crime and Rule Breaking*, 3rd edn. Oxford: Oxford University Press.

DVLA (2007) Driver and Vehicle Licensing Agency (www.dvla.gov.uk: accessed 28 February 2008).

DWP (2007) *Department for Work and Pensions* (www.dwp.gov.uk: accessed 24 September 2007).

Faqir, F. (2001) Intrafamily femicide in defence of honour: the case of Jordan, *Third World Quarterly*, 22(1): 65–82.

Federation Against Copyright Theft (2008) (www.fact-uk.org.uk: accessed 21 January 2008).

Fido, M. and Skinner, K. (1999) *The Official Encyclopedia of Scotland Yard*. London: Virgin Books.

Finney, A. (2006) *Domestic Violence, Sexual Assault and Stalking: Findings from the 2004/05 British Crime Survey*. Research, Development and Statistics Directorate, Home Office Online Report 12.

Flanagan, R. (2008) *Review of Policing: Final Report*. London: Home Office.

Furnell, S. (2007) Identity impairment: the problems facing victims of identity fraud, *Computer Fraud and Security*, 12: 6–11.

Geberth, V. J. (2006) *Practical Homicide Investigation: Tactics, Procedures and Forensic Techniques*, 4th edn. Boca Raton: CRC Press.

Grieve, J., Harfield, C. and MacVean, A. (2007) *Policing*. London: Sage Publications.

Gudjonsson, G. (1995) 'Fitness for interview' during police detention: a conceptual framework for forensic assessment, *Journal of Forensic Psychiatry and Psychology*, 6(1): 185–97.

Hannibal, M. and Mountford, L. (2002) *The Law of Criminal and Civil Evidence: Principles and Practice*. Essex: Pearson Education.

Harvey-Lintz, T. and Tidwell, R. (1997) Effects of the 1992 Los Angeles civil unrest: post traumatic stress disorder symptomatology among law enforcement officers, *The Social Science Journal*, 34(2): 171–83.

Henry, A. and Smith, D. (2007) *Transformations of Policing*. Aldershot: Ashgate Publishing Limited.

Highways Agency (2007) *Welcome to the Highways Agency.* (www.highways.gov.uk: accessed 10 October 2007).

HMCS (2007) *About Her Majesty's Courts Service* (www.hmcourts-service.gov.uk: accessed 21 February 2008).

HM Government (2007) *Joint Intelligence Committee (JIC)* (www.intelligence. gov.uk: accessed 19 February 2008).

Holmes, R. and Holmes, S. (1998) *Contemporary Perspectives on Serial Murder.* California: Sage Publications.

Home Office (2006a) *Research Development Statistics* (www.homeoffice.gov.uk/rds/ bcs1.html: accessed 22 December 2006).

Home Office (2006b) *Operational Policing: Prosecution Team Manual of Guidance –* 2004 Edition (www.police.homeoffice.gov.uk/operational-policing/prosecution-manual-guidance: accessed 22 February 2007).

Home Office (2007a) *Home Office: About Us* (www.homeoffice.gov.uk: accessed 16 October 2007).

Home Office (2007b) *Security: Terrorism and the Law* (www.homeoffice.gov.uk/ security/terrorism-and-the-law: accessed 29 February 2008).

HSE (2007) *Health and Safety Executive* (www.hse.gov.uk: accessed 15 October 2007).

Innes, M. (2003) *Investigating Murder: Detective Work and the Police Response to Criminal Homicide.* Oxford: Oxford University Press.

Jeffreys, A.J., Wilson, V. and Thein, S.L. (1985) Individual-specific 'fingerprints' of human DNA, *Nature,* 316: 76–9.

Jewkes, Y. (ed.) (2007) *Crime Online.* Cullompton: Willan.

Judicial Communications Office (2008) *Judiciary of England and Wales* (www.judiciary. gov.uk: accessed 8 March 2008).

Karmen, A. (2007) *Crime Victims: An Introduction to Victimology,* 6th edn. Belmont: Thomson Wadsworth.

Komarinski, P. (2005) *Automated Fingerprint Identification Systems (AFIS).* Burlington: Elsevier Academic Press.

Lane, B. (1992) *The Encyclopedia of Forensic Science.* London: Headline Book Publishing plc.

Langford, A., Dean, J., Reed, R., Holmes, D., Weyers, J. and Jones, A. (2005) *Practical Skills in Forensic Science.* Harlow: Pearson Education.

Liska, A., Lawrence, J. and Sanchirico, A. (1982) Fear of crime as a social fact, *Social Forces,* 60(3): 760–70.

Loader, I. and Mulcahy, A. (2003) *Policing and the Condition of England: Memory, Politics and Culture.* Oxford: Oxford University Press.

Lorentz, J., Hill, L. and Samimi, B. (2000) Occupational needlestick injuries in a Metropolitan Police Force, *American Journal of Preventive Medicine,* 18(2): 146–50.

MacPherson, W. (2007) The Stephen Lawrence inquiry, in E. McLaughlin (ed.) *The New Policing.* London: Sage Publications.

MAIB (2006) Marine Accident Investigation Branch (www.maib.gov.uk: accessed 20 December 2006).

Malcolm, J.L. (2002) *Guns and Violence: The English Experience.* Massachusetts: Harvard University Press.

McCartney, C. (2006) *Forensic Identification and Criminal Justice: Forensic Science, Justice and Risk.* Cullompton: Willan.

McLaughlin, E. (2007) *The New Policing.* London: Sage Publications.

Merritt, J. (2007) *Law for Student Police Officers.* Exeter: Learning Matters.

Met Office (2007) *PACRAM and CHEMET* (www.metoffice.gov.uk: accessed 20 June 2007).

Metropolitan Police Authority (2007) *Trident* (www.stoptheguns.org: accessed 9 February 2007).

NACRO (2004) *Who we are* (www.nacro.org.uk: accessed 29 January 2008).

NaCTSO (2007) *NaCTSO: National Counter Terrorism Security Office* (www.nactso. gov.uk: accessed 25 September 2007).

NCALT (2008) *NCALT: National Centre for Applied Learning Technologies* (www.ncalt.com: accessed 6 February 2008).

NCIS (2000) *The National Intelligence Model* (www.police.homeoffice.gov.uk/ news-and-publications/publication/operational-policing/nim-introduction: accessed 1 April 2008).

NCPE (2006) *Guidance on Policing Motorways.* Bedfordshire: National Centre for Policing Excellence.

Newburn, T. (2003) *Handbook of Policing.* Cullompton: Willan.

Newburn, T., Williamson, T. and Wright, A. (eds) (2007) *Handbook of Criminal Investigation.* Cullompton: Willan.

NSPCC (2006) *Help and Advice* (www.nspcc.org.uk: accessed 7 February 2008).

Pepper, I.K. (2005) *Crime Scene Investigation: Methods and Procedures.* Maidenhead: Open University Press.

Police National Legal Database (2005) Welcome to PNLD (www.pnld.co.uk: accessed 20 December 2006).

Povey, K. (2000) *On the Record: Thematic Inspection Report on Police Crime Recording, the Police National Computer and Phoenix Intelligence System Data Quality.* London: Her Majesty's Inspectorate of Constabulary.

RAIB (2007) *Rail Accident Investigation Branch* (www.raib.gov.uk: accessed 26 February 2007).

Ratcliffe, J. (ed.) (2004) *Strategic Thinking in Criminal Intelligence.* New South Wales: The Federation Press.

Rawlings, P. (2002) *Policing: A Short History.* Cullompton: Willan.

RCMP (2007) *Royal Canadian Mounted Police* (www.rcmp-grc.gc.ca: accessed 21 February 2008).

Reiner, R. (2000) *The Politics of the Police*, 3rd edn. Oxford: Oxford University Press.

Research, Development and Statistics (2007) *About RDS* (www.homeoffice.gov.uk/ rds: accessed 21 February 2008).

Rogers, C. and Lewis, R. (eds) (2007) *Introduction to Police Work*. Cullompton: Willan.

Rogers, M.D. (2003) Police force! An examination of the use of force, firearms and less-lethal weapons by British police, *Police Journal*, 76 (189).

RoSPA (2008) *The Royal Society for the Prevention of Accidents* (www.rospa.com: accessed 21 February 2008).

Sanders, A. and Young, R. (2007) *Criminal Justice*, 3rd edn. Oxford: Oxford University Press.

Schechter, H. and Everitt, D. (2006) *The A to Z Encyclopedia of Serial Killers*. New York: Pocket Books.

Scottish Police Services Authority (2008) *Expert Support for Scotland's Police and Criminal Justice Community* (www.spsa.police.uk: accessed 18 February 2008).

Security Industry Authority (2008) *Welcome to the SIA* (www.the-sia.org.uk/home: accessed 17 July 2008).

Sheptycki, J. (ed.) (2000) *Issues in Transnational Policing*. London: Routledge.

Skills for Justice (2008) *National Occupational Standards (NOS)* (www.skillsforjustice. com: accessed 29 April 2008).

Skolnick, J. (1966) *Justice Without Trial*. New York: Wiley.

Slapper, G. and Kelly, D. (2009) *The English Legal System*, 9th edn. Abingdon: Routledge-Cavendish.

SOCA (2006) *Serious Organized Crime Agency* (www.soca.gov.uk: accessed 15 March 2007).

The Crown Prosecution Service (2007) *Director of Public Prosecutions* (www.cps.gov.uk: accessed 25 September 2007).

Thomas, T. (2007) *Criminal Records: A Database for the Criminal Justice System and Beyond*. Hampshire: Palgrave Macmillan.

Thurman, J. (2006) *Practical Bomb Scene Investigation*. Boca Raton: CRC Press.

Touche Ross (1987) *Review of Scientific Support for the Police*, vol. III. London: Home Office.

Tullett, T. (1981) *Famous Cases of Scotland Yard's Murder Squad: From Crippen to the Black Panther*. London: Triad Grafton.

Tunnell, K.D. (1992) *Choosing Crime: The Criminal Calculus of Property Offenders*. Chicago: Nelson-Hall Inc.

UKBA (2008) UK Border Agency (www.ukba.homeoffice.gov.uk: accessed 29 April 2008).

UK Resilience (2007) *Introduction to the Civil Contingencies Secretariat* (www.ukresilience.info/ccs.aspx: accessed 20 September 2007).

Unison (2007) *About Us: Essential Information* (www.unison.org.uk: accessed 5 March 2008).

United Nations (2004) *Basic Fact about the United Nations* (www.un.org: accessed 5 March 2008).

Victim Support Scheme (2008) *Victim Support: How We Can Help You* (www.victimsupport.org.uk: accessed 28 February 2008).

Waddington, P.A.J. (1999) Police (canteen) sub-culture: an appreciation, *British Journal of Criminology*, 39(2): 287–309.

Walker, C. (2006) Clamping down on terrorism in the United Kingdom, *Journal of International Criminal Justice*, 4(5): 1137–51.

Warlow, T. (2005) *Firearms, the Law, and Forensic Ballistics*, 2nd edn. Boca Raton: CRC Press.

Weissman, B. (2002) Corrosives training, *Occupational Health & Safety*, 71(9): 160.

Williams, R. and Johnson, P. (2008) *Genetic Policing: The Use of DNA in Criminal Investigations*. Cullompton: Willan.

Wolodarsky-Franke, A. and Lara, A. (2005) The role of 'forensic' dendrochronology in the conservation of alerce (Fitzroya cupressoides ((Molina) Johnston)) forests in Chile. *Dendrochronologia*, 22(3): 235–40.

Wright, J. (2006) The importance of Europe in the global campaign against terrorism, *Terrorism and Political Violence*, 18: 281–99.

WRVS (2007) *Make It Count: What We Do* (www.wrvs.org.uk: accessed 14 February 2008).